Guide to Athletic Recruiting & Career Education

Guide to Athletic Recruiting & Career Education

Be a student of the Game

Written for student—athletes, coaches,
parents and counselors

Coach Lisimba Patilla, MBA-PMP

www.noblesteps.com

Library of Congress Control Number: 2010901194
ISBN: Hardcover   978-1-4500-2846-2
               Softcover   978-1-4500-2845-5
               Ebook   978-1-4500-2847-9

This book was printed in the United States of America.

To order additional copies of this book, contact:
Xlibris Corporation
1-888-795-4274
www.Xlibris.com
Orders@Xlibris.com
73935

CONTENTS

SECTION I

SECTION II

SECTION III

> True progress in any field is a
> relay race and not a single event.
> —Cavett Roberts

THE AUTHOR

Lisimba Patilla, MBA is a former student-athlete and scholarship recipient at Northwood University, a NCAA Division II powerhouse in Midland, Michigan where he started two years at cornerback. Lisimba comes from three generations of student-athletes to have been awarded athletic scholarships: uncle, nephews, cousins and him. He has rare first hand experience as to what athletes, parents and coaches deal with in the world of recruiting and can speak to all of their needs.

He educates parents, coaches and players on the facts and myths about recruiting, how to be recruited and recruiting and career promotional methods. Before Noblesteps Management, Lisimba spent 11 years as the liaison between junior colleges and small businesses in Chicago, Cleveland, Toledo and Erie, PA employing education and training portfolios and developing prospect pools for businesses. His athletic recruiting and career firm now builds bridges to Division 1, 2, 3 and NAIA schools and provides an opportunity for student-athletes to be evaluated for athletic – scholarship both as a student and as an athlete. Noblesteps Management, is insuring he is a team player in providing coaches at all levels the right student-athletes for their universities and reducing the likelihood of student-athletes transferring, dropping out or changing majors. Furthermore, increasing the possibility student-athletes turn pro in something other than sports, as the NCAA promotes.

> The Harder you Work the
> Harder it is to Surrender
> —Vince Lombardi

Acknowledgements

First I would like to thank God for making the introspection, ideal, writing, printing, and publishing of this manuscript possible; without Him nothing is possible. Second, I would like to thank the brave men and women of our armed forces who have or will fight valiantly to secure our freedom in this great country against those who wish to do us harm. Last, I want to thank my ancestors who came before me; those whom I stand on their shoulders with the hopes and dreams of building a brighter future for my family and student-athletes with aspirations of a bright future on and off the field of play. Moreover, a special thanks to my loving wife Tamika who is the firm, yet gentle foundation of the Patilla family. I love you so much. Your patience and support makes this manuscript special because you supported and encouraged me the entire way. As I look back at the road I have traveled to get to this point, my mom, dad, sister, brother, uncles, aunts, grandparents, and cousins are all reserved special thanks for playing a role in my development as a person of usefulness. I also want to thank all the student-athletes I have coached over the years that help confirm that there is truly a need for leadership in athletics. I hope they believe they are better people because of our interactions. Also, thanks to the college career directors and college coaches who took the time out of their schedules to answer survey questions and contribute to the research it took to create this book. Noblesteps Management LLC is a recruiting, education company with the mission of "Raising the Bar of Student-Athlete Recruiting Education". Noblesteps Management's Athletic Recruiting Guide is another noble step at providing student-athletes with not only the realities of recruiting, or how to be recruited, but with the resources to be a student-athlete for life and compete on and off the field; differentiating themselves from the pack in sport and profession. It can be said that sports is a short term exercise in character building, recruiting is a short term exercise in exposure and evaluation, and a career is a lifelong fulfilling marathon in being useful. I hope that everyone who reads Noblesteps Management's Athletic Recruiting Guide feels that I have provided them something that is useful in their lives.

Introduction

As I am writing this guidebook and done my research, I have found that many other authors focus solely on athletic recruiting as though the student-athlete is an athlete student. That irresponsibility is found in guidebook after guidebook whereas authors commit an oversight of not providing student-athletes with functional tools and perspectives that not only serve their athletic recruiting education needs, but their career education needs. If you take a moment and stop to consider that the probability of a student-athlete making it to the professional level is less than 1%, why would an ex-coach, player, or businessman ever write a book that ignores 99% of student-athletes? I can't answer that question, but I can say that the 99% of student-athletes that go on to college often share the following five goals:

1) Being confident in your college selection
2) Earn playing time in college
3) Earn scholarship aid to offset the cost of attendance
4) Minimize and/or eliminate the need for student loan debt
5) Graduate college, motivated to pursue a career path

This Noblesteps Guide is the result of years of experiences, research, surveys, and casual conversations with college coaches, college career directors, high school coaches, parents and former student-athletes to create a responsible athletic recruiting guidebook that stays TRUE to the coaching philosophy that "it is more than a game". I share the belief, as many successful athletic coaches share, that although the game is played with talented players, success is based on if they believe I made a positive contribution to their lives outside of the field of play and they are a better person because of it. Therefore, my writings will cover everything a student-athlete needs to know to be recruited for a sport for college; all the what, whys and how's.

Moreover, it will provide practical approaches for parents, student-athletes, and coaches to use to be their own recruiting coordinators and promote themselves and/or student-athletes in a professional and thorough manner.

Finally, this manuscript casts a perspective on how those actions can and should be carried over into pursuing a professional life outside the field of play and why it is important to hone your skills as an athlete; equally important is to have a vision of what life can be like when the sports experience has run its course. I know of NO other manuscript that responsibly provides a system or methodology for developing an athletic recruiting plan; stories of successful student-athletes and all the processes that can reappear in your future professional goals. Less than 1% of all athletes make it to the professional level. Therefore, I thought it to be **irresponsible to write a manuscript dedicated ONLY to athletic recruiting**. As the NCAA promotes, and I thoroughly support, there are opportunities for young adults to pursue professions in something other than sports. Throughout this manuscript you will find plenty of data to support developing a career plan that parallels your recruiting plan. You are not only recruited to play the sport of your dreams, but when the game is over and the lights are off on athletics, you have begun an educational path that is lighted by your energy and motivation to make a difference in that profession. A student-athlete is a student first! And although college coaches recruit athletes on talent, then academics; all student-athletes should be aware that if colleges know who you are and believe you can help their collegiate teams, they will pick you as a future member of it. Unfortunately you won't decide which one picks you. The same is true in careers; companies need to know about you to consider you for a position (unless you have a family business). The more businesses know who you are and what experience you bring to the table, the better. In the end, often the company picks you up and if it is a good fit for you, you accept. If you are a blue chip athlete you must know that at some point as a result of athletic peaking, injury or both, your day in sports will end and you need to have a plan to enter the recruiting arena to serve in the job market. This guidebook will provide you with all the tools to create your plan for athletic and career recruiting that can provide you with the long term perspective you need to navigate the competitive collegiate recruiting and occupational landscape. I have said it many times; athletic recruiting is the biggest decision a young adult makes early in their lives. How you go about recruiting is about discovering, preparing, and executing a plan to be in a pool of athletes, whereas you are chosen as a beneficiary of a college scholarship aid package to a college or university. The fact is your academic career will last much longer than your athletic career. Therefore, not only is it important to be in a pool of athletes, but to also recognize how to get into pools of potential employers and where to position yourself with a career that will last throughout your working life.

The following stories are about student-athletes who had a vision of short term athletic greatness and long term educational identity. The Noblesteps Recruiting Guide uncovers the mystery of athletic recruiting and provides the information, resources, and a dynamic model to assist student-athletes, parents, and coaches on how to take full advantage of the opportunities provided by athletics and recruiting. This has become so important that the NCAA's newest reform centerpiece of college sports teams is the **Academic Progress Rate** to improve graduation rates of "student-athletes." As a result, schools are judged by sport on a baseline of minimum expected graduation and retention rates and those who are unable to meet those baselines are penalized. The penalties include loss of scholarships, potential probation, and exclusion from post season tournaments. College coaches can lose their jobs if APR's decline and it sets an unwritten rule that coaches should not recruit athletes on talent alone; instead the combination of talent and academic potential should be considered. Student-athletes should not only focus on athletic talent but developing good study habits to serve them academically and a career plan that compliments their academic practices. The following success stories of real student-athletes will provide you with all the intangible principles of being a student-athlete in a competitive global job market. I enjoy reading stories of ex-college players who talk about how they are better people because of their college coach; I urge ALL parents and student-athletes to consider that as a point of emphasis into how you discern if a college coach cares about your future as a person of usefulness beyond their program.

SECTION I

Athletic Recruiting Education

Do you know the difference between the facts and the myths of recruiting?

In this section you will learn the following:

- ✓ What recruiting is and what it is not
- ✓ How to get prepared as a student-athlete
- ✓ How to sell yourself
- ✓ What college coaches are looking for
- ✓ The major role of parenting
- ✓ How to manage the recruiting process

To see far is one thing; going there is another

Often when you collaborate with others, it is a win-win position

Anytime you make choices founded on solid life values, then you are in a better position to sustain your level of commitment

Ordinary people with commitment can make an extraordinary impact on their world

—John C. Maxwell

Two Recruits

Two recruits wanted to be recruited for a college scholarship and have a career after college. Both young men had good grades, ACT scores, athletic abilities, and positive personalities. They both decided to increase the chances of winning a scholarship by praying to God to receive a scholarship offer from a college coach. However, one of the recruits prepared to receive a scholarship by marketing himself to college coaches, attending camps and combines, taking career assessments, and investigating academic scholarship aid; the other recruit thought he was good enough and God would answer his prayers. Which recruit are YOU?

The True Story of a Competitive Student-Athlete Jessica Toochech

Jessica Toochech never imagined that one day she would be playing professional softball for the Akron Racers. In fact, Jessica as a young lady from Medina, OH never imagined that she would even play high school softball because she thought it was too hard. Furthermore, she thought that college softball was an unrealistic goal. When she finally did play in high school and was convinced by her coach that she could play at the next level, she prepared a highlight video and sent it off to area colleges. She was rejected by most schools and by the end of the recruiting process Jessica ended up with a partial scholarship to Kent-State University. She recalled being devastated that her hard work did not produce a full ride scholarship. Jessica kept working hard until her junior year when she earned the full ride that she always wanted. She recalled thinking how she was the best at her high school, but just another player in college. She attributes her success to the adversity of competition that pushed her to step up and rise to the professional level. Jessica believes being a student-athlete means school first! There is going to be a day when athletics stop and you will need education as a student to carry you for the rest of your life. Jessica lives by the words she speaks. She graduated from Kent State with a degree in Special Education and works as a 7th and 8th grade Intervention Specialist for Special Education. She now calls on her learning experiences as a student-athlete to focus on the little things, do things right the first time, and have a sense of priority and responsibility to meet guidelines with those whom she is responsible for. Jessica urges current and future student-athletes to not overlook the little things as a student and athlete because it creates a good habit that will serve you in your career when athletics has run its course.

A Spirited Story in Recruiting Education—Ahmad Sanders

Recruiting is different for every sport and every person. One of the biggest keys is selling yourself as a student-athlete, getting the job done as a student and athlete, and then communicating that to as many coaches in the country as possible. Often times parents find that their son/daughter from a measurable point of view fall short of the norms and determine that in order to insure that their student-athlete gets noticed, they hire a recruiting service. That is what Sam Sanders of Flint, Michigan did for his son Ahmad in 1993. Ahmad was an undersized football player at 5'2", weighing 123 pounds at Northern High School as well as a diminutive sized wrestler, to the human eye, of course. However, when his high school football coach named an award after him for future football players to receive at Northern High School, people quickly understood that the Ahmad A. Sanders Heart & Soul Award was a foot print for future players to step into and a distinguishable attribute to a student-athlete who was uncertain what his college future would look like. Ahmad wrestled with some of Michigan's best wrestlers, many of whom were on his wrestling team and went on to wrestle at the collegiate level. Ahmad was not all jock! He graduated from Northern High School with a 3.87 GPA and was a two time state champion. Ahmad attended Central Michigan University on a scholarship and his father attributes his accomplishment to both his hard work and the fact he used a recruiting service to get his name out to college coaches. Ahmad attributed his success to his parents who he felt instilled the importance of education and putting in the effort to be all he could be in the classroom. He noticed that teachers in high school were impressed with his efforts and applauded a student that was concerned about their academic success. Ahmad exemplified what being a student-athlete is all about.

However, he did not rest once he made it to college; he kept up the effort as a student and as an athlete. By the time he graduated from CMU, he had finished 2nd, 3rd and 4th in the MAC in wrestling, was voted team captain in 2001 and qualified for nationals where he finished 9th and two seconds from being an All-American.

Ahmad recalled his All-American shortfall as a reminder of how quickly you can be distracted from reaching your goals and your goal can slip away. He says, regardless of his athletic successes and shortfalls, those achievements are diminutive and can always be devalued, unlike his educational accomplishments. Ahmad completed his college career with a 3.1 GPA and a degree in Health Fitness and Rehabilitation and a Minor in Nutrition. He utilizes his passion for fitness and well being to encourage doctors in Michigan to buy pharmaceuticals from the company he works for where he ranks as one of the top representatives in the country. Ahmad stays competitive, but says he allows the student in him to continue to learn what needs to be done to be successful. He considers himself a spirited student-athlete who believes athletics taught him how to be a team player, but still separates himself from others and resists the intoxicating urge to be mediocre.

Defining recruiting?

Recruiting is generating a pool of talented athletes to compete at an institution. This is usually for high schools, colleges and is used to refer to entities that recruit in all sectors of occupations as well. The process of what you focus on and spend your energy doing is what will be discussed in this guidebook; how colleges accumulate pools of athletes and what you can do to insure you are in the pool and stand out from the rest. Furthermore, it is difficult to qualify recruiting totally; this book will provide you with functional courses of action to effectively develop recruiting plans for your athletic and career aspirations. Important aspects of recruiting for collegiate recruiting budgets is that they are not made of monopoly money and they have limits based on revenue producing sports like men's football and basketball versus all other men's sports and women's sports. Therefore, it will be your responsibility to know the rules, play the game, and get your name, achievements, abilities and goals in front of the coaches for evaluation. One thing all potential student-athletes should know is the facts; to be able to differentiate them from the myths.

Know Recruiting Myths from Facts

There are quite a few myths that can derail your recruiting hopes. Educating your self is key.

    ✓ **Myth**: Great players always get recruited

✓ **Fact:** This is only true for the players who are ranked, who has been all-state for two years, and attend all the invite only combines as well as being ranked in all the magazines and recruiting boards. If you are only great one year in high school—fewer college coaches know your name and as a consequence you run the risk of not being recruited.

✓ **Myth**: You are supposed to wait until your senior year to start the recruiting process.

✓ **Fact:** No, you should start the recruiting process as early as possible because you build relationships with coaches and become familiar with the type of college and degree program you want to pursue.

✓ **Myth**: If you are good enough they will find you.

✓ **Fact:** Maybe if you are a 6'6", 320 pound offensive tackle who just played his first year in football. If you are 5'10", 166, talented QB, and good enough to play at the next level, probably not. You will need to work to get your name out to coaches. College coaching budgets are larger for the revenue producing sports and smaller for the non-revenue producing sports. Furthermore, division I budgets are much larger than division II budgets. Therefore, it is imperative to get your information in front of coaches so that you can be evaluated versus their teams needs.

✓ **Myth**: It is up to the high school coach to get me recruited

✓ **Fact:** If you have a high school coach who is active in the recruiting process, you are lucky. Most high school coaches are teachers, therefore not having the time or the budget to perform all the duties necessary for recruiting. However, coaches should be available to provide letters of recommendations for players, return phone calls from coaches about players, and give players feedback on the level they believe student-athletes can play at.

✓ **Myth:** If mom or dad puts pressure on my high school coach he will get me recruited

✓ **Fact:** This usually works just the opposite of the intended act. If you want your coach to help you with recruiting, ask for a letter of recommendation. Again, coaches at the high school level are predominantly teachers.

✓ Demanding that they sacrifice time with their families to perform recruiting duties that you can do at home is a lot to ask.

✓ **Myth:** I am competing for a scholarship against student-athletes that are my age, my size and my experience

✓ **Fact:** You are competing for a scholarship against other high school players who have spent a year or two in junior college, or who may be transferring from other division I or II schools. This is why it is so important to develop yourself to be the best you can be.

✓ **Myth**: Since I have the best grades, I am certain to get an athletic scholarship

✓ **Fact**: Grades are very important in the recruiting process; however, teams with the best mix of talent are often the most competitive. Therefore, coaches work miracles with their admission offices to get players with low grades into their universities. Furthermore, if that is still not enough, coaches may "grey shirt" (players sit out the first semester of college).

Recruiting Guides for the NCAA, NAIA & NJCAA

Following are all the resources regardless of what division you are pursuing that are FREE and provided by athletic associations for your use in guiding you through the recruiting game. This information is particularly important in defining what needs to be acted on to qualify for different divisions and associations of college athletics:

The NCAA Guide for the College Bound Student-Athlete
The National Collegiate Athletic Association—*www.ncaa.org*
P.O. Box 6222, Indianapolis, IN 46206—888.388.9748
The NAIA Guide for the College Bound Student-Athlete
National Association of Intercollegiate Athletics—*www.naia.org*
1200 Grand Boulevard, Kansas City, MO 64106—816.595.8000
The NJCAA Guide for the College bound Student-Athlete
National Junior College Athletic Association—*www.njcaa.org*
1755 Telstar Drive, Suite 103-719.590.9788
Colorado Springs, CO 80920

These resources are adjusted on an annual basis. Therefore rules, scholarships, awards, evaluations, phone contacts, and signing dates tend to change along with these guides. I strongly recommend you order new ones on a yearly basis.

NCAA Eligibility Center
Website: *www.eligibilitycenter.org/*
Toll-Free Number: 877.262.1492

To receive any type of financial aid: scholarships of any kind (athletic or academic) and be able to play or practice at the NCAA Division I or II level, you must be registered. We suggest this is done at the beginning of the student-athletes' junior year of high school. The cost is $60.00. There are 16 core classes that must be completed for division I and 14 for division II.

Matter of Fact

As a matter of fact, there are a couple truths that hold true for what I estimate to be 99% of student athletes that don't have a bag full of hats to choose from on national television or at an arranged signing ceremony.

- ✓ There are many **forms of scholarship** aid available to student-athletes, roughly thousands. Superior performance, measurable potential, plus exposure get an athlete ranked above others and usually produce athletic scholarship offers. Ultimately, it comes down to marketing, exposure, and being represented in as many recruiting pools as possible. Furthermore, once you start getting offers, it is important to not jump the gun and continue to wait for more offers. Therefore, especially at the division II and NAIA level, you will have negotiation leverage to ask for more scholarship aid.
- ✓ Athletic opportunities to continue playing sports is **80-20** for Division I. This means that **20%** of the opportunities exist at the **Division I** level and the remaining opportunities are at Division II, III, NAIA, and NJCAA.
- ✓ **The numbers game** is an immensely important attribute of recruiting on and off the field. Your success can be directly attributed to how many colleges you are involved with. As offers start to come, it provides you with leverage to negotiate between colleges to insure you don't leave money on the table.
- ✓ **Start researching early.** Building a recruiting and career plan is not a one day homework assignment; it runs concurrently throughout a student—athlete's secondary, post-secondary, and graduate years. You will continuously be redefining your goals to take advantage of opportunities as they arise. The athletic recruiting process is too dynamic and important to wait until your senior year to start; and that goes for your career planning as well. The early bird gets the first worm!

- ✓ You can find a college that provides the academic and athletic **opportunities** for you as long as you understand that it may not be a household name or the school that your parents attended.
- ✓ The true purpose of your **high school coach** in the recruiting process is to provide you with an assessment of where they think you can play (Division I, II, III, junior college). They are also good in providing you with letters of recommendation about what you meant to their sports program in high school. This is an awesome piece to help sell you to coaches as a solid recruit. Beyond that it is not their responsibility to get you recruited, so don't wait on them, be proactive.
- ✓ If you are getting mail and phone calls from a **college coach**, don't assume that it means you are high on their list of recruits. They may be just being courteous. The **BEST** way I know to realize where you stand with a coach is to **ASK.**

Life Changing Event

Your decision on the college you choose, the major you choose, and how long it takes you to accomplish the steps in between, is the process of changing your life. I strongly suggest you take this very serious. Conversations with people who have walked a similar path; coaches, parents, and guidance counselors are immensely important to gain confidence in your final decision. Make a list of priorities that begin and end with education; athletics is what you do in between the time you are pursuing a career. Furthermore, athletics can help you to reveal the character you need to succeed in life and in your career.

What are College Coaches looking for in Student-Athletes?

- ✓ **Academics. Grades. Core courses complete. ACT/SAT scores**. Because of the NCAA APR (Academic Progress Rate), college coaches are less inclined to push hard for a student-athlete who they don't feel can do the work in college. Therefore, when a coach has to choose between a good vs. average student, there is a good chance they will choose the student-athlete with the better grades.

✓ **Sport Performance** is obviously a big contributor to what measurement a college coach looks at when considering a student-athlete. There are some caveats to this measurement if the athlete is from a smaller high school, but then the coach looks at their other measurables like speed and size. By performing well you provide yourself with a good possibility to be chosen. The eye in the sky does not lie. When a coach evaluates your film and you do well, it bodes well for you.

✓ **Potential** is another determinant to coaches because they are not totally recruiting you from where you are as a student-athlete. They are recruiting you from where they think you can be in a year or two of collegiate weight training and competition.

✓ **Work ethic** is another evaluation variable that usually comes from the high school coach's letter of recommendation, but also comes from watching how you perform on film. They will observe how you hustle during plays and look at how you have improved physically from year to year in strength and times.

✓ **Versatility** can be a double positive if when you compete in your sport you are able to play at a high level at more than one position and do it with a positive disposition. Colleges recruit based on the need of their sports team. Therefore, if your favorite position is not being recruited for, but you also compete well at the second or third position, it is possible to be recruited at that position. This is why being a team player on your sports team can help your team and your chances of being awarded a college scholarship.

✓ **Leadership** can be a huge evaluation point for college coaches. How you respond to adversity, (bad plays), how you treat your teammates, how you act towards referees, and how you act towards your coach. These actions are imperative points of reference to evaluate what type of teammate you will be in college and represent their university or college.

✓ **Athletic Diversity** is your ability to play more than one sport and do those sports well, especially in a complimentary fashion. Football and track, basketball and track, soccer and basketball. College coaches evaluate athletic ability and by increasing the frequency of competition, do it well and improve at it over time. College coaches can evaluate you from a broad perspective of potential, work ethic, versatility and athletic diversity.

Recruiting Wisdom

Give yourself the best opportunity to receive a written offer from a college coach by being involved with every coach in any division. For example, if your college coach tells you that they believe you are a Division II athlete, I suggest developing and sending a recruiting promotion about yourself to every Division II, III and NAIA school in the nation. That would make up about roughly 4000 schools and would increase your odds of being recruited and offered a scholarship.

✓ Recruiting Questionnaires from colleges is an attempt by the college to gather information about you. Don't underestimate how important this is to getting into the pool of athletes. You don't necessarily need to fill it out as long as you have an athletic resume that you can staple to it and send back. What is important is that you return it. Furthermore, calling the coach and following up with them to find out where you stand is not an unrealistic request.

✓ I love hearing the stories about college coaches and phone contact. However, I find that student-athletes are often not utilizing the conversation as they should. Instead, they allow the coach to give them a college sales speech rather than discussing the following meat and potatoes of any recruiting discussion:

○ Ask them if they have evaluated your game video and for their assessment
○ Ask them if they intend to bring you down for an "official visit"
○ Ask them if they plan on visiting you and your family

✓ Make sure you know who you are talking to. Sometimes students are talking to a graduate assistant and assume they are a decision maker like a head or assistant coach. Coaches are salesmen for the university and often like to persuade players to come in and join their team as a "preferred walk-on". I prefer you ignore these requests and move on to schools that you have a better opportunity to play for. Before your senior year in high school make as many visits to Division I, II, and III colleges as you can. The purpose is to get a feel for what the college experience is all about. Understand how admissions work and what campus opportunities are available.

Furthermore, determine if you want to attend a college in a rural or urban area. All of this is important to find a college that is the right fit for you.

○ *www.college-visits.com* provides a complete list of college tours and originating cities.

Talk to your High School Football Coach

Your football coach needs to know your aspirations if he is unaware of them. By knowing your goals and objectives he can provide you with recommendations and possibly complete letters of recommendation for college coaches that he believes would be a good fit for you. This prepares him to know he will possibly be receiving inquiries from colleges about you and keeps your coach in the loop as schools begin to contact him. Furthermore, Noblesteps Management provides an athletic recruiting system whereas our web-based athletic resumes can embed your coach(s) letter(s) of recommendation(s). High school coaches who are also teachers find themselves with parents and student-athletes with high expectations of what they should be doing about recruiting. Although recruiting is a parent or student-athlete's responsibility, noblesteps.com can assist coaches in streamlining this very time-consuming process.

Story of Parenting & Promoting Top Tier Student-Athletes

Anthony and Tawana both had dreams as youth of playing college sports. Anthony succeeded as an offensive lineman at Florida A & M. After Anthony and Tawana married, they made a pact to not only love each other but to support their children in sports and provide every opportunity for them to play college sports if they wished. Their first son could play an abundance of positions well in football. They made sure he attended all the top tier athletic combines, camps and tournaments to provide him the opportunity to be exposed to and evaluated by coaches. By his senior year he had three "Big Ten" offers and three MAC offers for football. Tawana and Anthony stayed diligent in their goal of keeping their children active and exposed to college coaches. Their middle child, an interior lineman earned first team all state his senior year. He also went all state in the shot put and discus in track and field as a junior and was awarded a full scholarship to play college football

Tawana says it is important to keep young people focused through sports. That focus has much to do with preparing to go to combines and camps to perform well. She also stressed academics; GRADES, GRADES, GRADES, whereas if their young men did not give their best efforts in their books, they were easily absent from a sports contest. Anthony and Tawana say, "It is important to work together as a family, be cheerleaders for kids at games, and stay out of the way of coaches." Furthermore, they stress a deep faith in God and a belief that their sons should stay humble in their on the field achievements and diligent in getting better as individuals, athletes, and future professionals. They believe recruiting to be a family affair with a lot of hard work, time, and energy to be prepared for those opportunities when they knock.

Five Most Counterproductive Parenting Acts

1. Telling them you would be disappointed in them if their efforts fall short in sports, recruiting or life. This is done often directly or indirectly by parents as a direct correlation to the stress and competition that affects families and student-athletes during recruiting or competitive contests of sport teams or individual sports. The idea of communicating disappointment to student-athletes is to motivate the student-athlete to inspire them to reach higher. However, the parents' role is to motivate and be a support system to a student-athlete and it is imperative to their success that you let them know you love them regardless of what happens on the field or sports arena.

2. Relive your athletic life through your child in a way that puts pressure on them to perform. Living vicariously through a son or daughter has been going on since the beginning of time. Telling your son or daughter athlete about how you handled a situation with a sport that you played seems on the surface as a perfect way to motivate them to perform in the sport they are currently playing. However, your enthusiasm as a parent may not be mutually shared by your child. As a result, this type of well-meaning encouragement may contribute to your son or daughter feeling inferior. They may be happy by playing a more team oriented role, whereas you may have been the star of the team. Sometimes athletes are like flowers; blooming at different periods of life. As a result, reliving your success through them may inhibit the growth of an aspiring student-athlete.

3. Compete with the coach on every decision the coaches make that effect your son/daughter's playing time or recruiting expectation. This is one role that I see most often on teams with losing records or at the losing end of a contest. Our society is very judgmental and we all want the best for our children. We occasionally believe that if we push coaches in the direction that benefits our child we are creating a better circumstance for them and their lives. I believe the antithesis of this. I have experienced first-hand, student-athletes who expect life to give them the opportunities that their parents pushed on coaches. Furthermore, the coach may develop resentment towards the family and student-athlete or other team members may begin to treat the student-athlete differently. It is unlikely that trying to coerce a coach to doing what you want works, but it can be very counterproductive to your child, their team, and the coach in the short and long run.

4. Overtly compare your son/daughter's skills, ability or attitude to other players on the team. This can result in a student-athlete who feels they are not loved by the parent because they are not good enough to live up to a standard set by someone their own age that they know personally. Comparing your son or daughter to another player they know can be very counter-productive to their development as a person as well as a student-athlete.

5. Approach competition and adversity as counterproductive acts in your child's development. This can be a huge mistake for many parents. Helicopter parents like me and many others only want the best for our kids and we hover around them in protection mode hoping to derail anything that in our protective minds will directly challenge our child's dreams. Many times competition and adversity is improving on what coaches believe will develop the athlete as a person and as a player. As a coach, I believe that these elements of sport are what make the playing field a level one, because to succeed we often need to experience and effectively handle the challenges that accompany competition and adversity.

How to get evaluated by college coaches

Camps, Clinics & Combines are great sources to showcase your athletic ability to coaches. The camps that have a large number of college coaches in attendance are much better than summer camps that are limited only to coaches from the college. My research of camps (example—Michigan, Ohio State) reflected that the larger camps usually bring in coaches from the region to help run the camps and therefore evaluate players which provide a huge platform for a student-athlete to go from player zero to player hero!

AAU, Junior Olympics or Club Teams are great because they provide an opportunity to compete around in the sport you love. Furthermore, college coaches often attend club games to evaluate top players.

Recruiting Websites are something that all players who are interested in playing college sports should take advantage of. These sites are FREE and certainly should not be overlooked, they may not produce instant results and very little produces instant or guaranteed results except being the biggest, fastest and best player in your sport and being ranked as the Best in your sport with the grades to be eligible.

Recruiting packages are immensely important to get evaluated and will be discussed in-depth in the following chapters. Athletic resumes are a compilation of your athletic measurables, statistics, academic and athletic achievements. Furthermore it provides contact information of you, your coaches, where you attended school, what conference and division you play in. If you are really savvy with technology, you can build yourself a website or online athletic resume to provide an exclusive source of your achievements for colleges to evaluate. Moreover, a resume or athletic resume is not complete without a cover letter or opening letter. This provides the coach with an introduction of who you are and what your plans are as a student-athlete from an academic and career perception. Furthermore, it should be addressed to the coach personally as coaches appreciate when an athlete shows interest in their program. This approach to getting evaluated is useful especially if you start early!

The Recruiting Promotional Package

Developing a recruiting package for coaches is an important step to be evaluated by a college coach. The recruiting package has within it an athletic resume which is similar to a professional job resume except it encompasses predominantly athletic related achievements, measurables, goals, academic achievements, school and family information. The purpose is to provide the coach with the same information that they would find on the questionnaires that they send out. Most times when you receive an athletic questionnaire, it is best to attach your athletic resume to it and return it to the coach. There are two **Types of Athletic Résumé's:** one is where it is developed from a Microsoft word document and it can be provided as an attachment to an email or printed out and mailed to a coach. The other type of athletic resume is the web-based athletic resume which can be created two different ways. The first is by utilizing a web-based software like you can find at *www. visualcv.com.* On this web-site you can create an athletic resume and have your own personal URL for coaches to view your accomplishments and measurables. The cost for this is free. If you choose to add services there is a cost to upgrade. The advantage that a web-based athletic resume has over a word document is that it can have a live feed to video versus a Word document having limited capacity. Noblesteps.com creates VisualCV's for their clients and emails them to every school in Division I, II, III and NAIA to increase the odds of being evaluated, recruited and awarded an athletic scholarship by a collegiate university. The software also provides the means to not only build a resume, but the ability to watch videos via the resume through you tube and be printed as a PDF document that can be mailed to coaches that send you questionnaires. The other form of athletic résumé's is actually building a website to promote your child's accomplishments. Building a website is very useful as well, because again it provides the capacity to view more visual characteristics with pictures, videos and any other information that contributes to your son/daughter's image as a student-athlete. To compliment the athletic VisualCV and/or website, all submissions to coaches should encompass a cover letter or **promotional letter** as an introduction to the coach. Include your academic and athletic achievements and express how you would like to be a part of their program. These letters should be addressed directly to the coach with their name on it, because it shows that you as a student-athlete have done your homework on their program. Furthermore, the cover letter should express your interest in a career path and curriculum that is available at their school. Following is an example of an athletic resume & promotional letter:

Sample Promotional letter

James Doe
Anywhere USA
My Phone Number
My email address

Date

Dear Coach Scholarship

My name is James Doe and I am a junior at Mostly Winning High School where I am a running back on our football team.

I am extremely interested in learning more about your university and playing sports for your program. I feel that my athletic and academic talents and ability match your program and would be a great fit. In school I currently have a 3.9 GPA and a 32 ACT and I am interested in studying engineering. Furthermore, I finished 2009 1st team All State.

Thank you for your time and consideration. I look forward to speaking with you about the opportunity to play for your university. Feel free to contact Monday-Friday between the hours 6-8 PM.

A copy of my athletic resume can be viewed and printed by clicking on the following link:

www.visualcv.com/jamesdoe

Sincerely,

Scholarship Hopeful
My Contact Phone Number

Sample Web-Based Athletic Resume

View My VisualCV Online: http://www.visualcv.com/scholarshiphopeful

James Doe
Class of 2012
Phone 000-000-0000
Athlete/Sports
Parents: Love & Faith Hopeful

Athletic Measurables
Sports shot & Highlights

Measurables
Height: 5' 9"
Weight: 185
40 Yd.: 4.2
20Yd. Shuttle: 4.0
Bench max: 365
Squat max: 450

Athletic Resume

Season Highlights

GPA: 3.9 **ACT:** 32 (Honor Roll 4 years)

Registered for NCAA Clearing house: Yes
2009 Statistics

Carries	Yards	TD
182	1800	20

2008 Statistics

Carries	Yards	TD
78	800	9

Achievements
2009 1ˢᵗ Team All State
2008 2ⁿᵈ team All Conference

Scholarship Hopeful
Class 2012
Most Winning High School
Running back # 4
000-000-0000

Click once to watch embedded
Click twice to watch through
Youtube

High School Information

Northeast Ohio Conference—Division 1
Coach Jimmy Dean
Mostly Winning High School
Anywhere USA
(000) 000-0000
Pro-Style Offense
Desired Major(s): Business or Sports Management

Types of Promotional Videos

Coaches will request three types of promotional videos; **Skills Video, Highlight V ideo** or **Game Video**. Additional editing can be helpful to a college coach in evaluating your highlight video. Editing that can be helpful is anything that points to you before a play begins, a scrolling phrase that describes what is about to happen and an introductory opening explaining who you are and what you want to study in college. Regardless of the type of film you choose to develop, it is helpful to have a **game film** or your best games handy for coaches per their request. Therefore, when you send it to a college coach, they can evaluate not only how well you play, but how you respond to your mistakes, how hard you hustle, how you act towards referees during not so complimentary calls, and how you treat your teammates. In either case, your high school coach will need to provide you with a copy of the video and you will need to make additional copies. Ensure that you send the video DVD's with all your information: name, jersey color and number, phone number, and name of school. The **highlight film** is made up of clips of your best plays. This provides the coach or Recruiting Coordinator with a good look into what you do well. Some coaches want game film, others want highlight films, and some want **skills videos.** A skills video is a showcase of you executing pertinent sport related skills for the coach to evaluate. Different sports and various positions usually contribute to what type of video the coach will request in order to determine whether they want to add you to their pool of athletes. Therefore, it is important that you contact as many colleges as possible and increase the odds that a coach requests information like game, skill or highlight videos.

Promotional Schedule

In Season promoting of your game results is useful for their evaluation. You should make it a point to send coaches emails to promote your success as an update on your personal web page or VisualCV. Furthermore, plan on always updating your stats in the **Off Season** and sending that information to coaches as a summary of how well you performed and/or improved over the season. Also, it can be helpful to communicate to coaches how well you performed at camps, combines or showcases in the off season as a way to show improvement in times, strength or other related measurements.

It can be helpful to student-athletes, parents, and coaches to establish an in and off season promotional schedule to keep coaches apprised on the performance and improvement of student-athletes.

Social Media Marketing

YouTube is a web-based site that offers consumers a free, no-charge platform to upload videos up to 10 minutes in length. Youtube is a great place to upload your game or highlight videos. Furthermore, by adding your name to the video, search engines will find your name and if a coach is performing due diligence on what your virtual image is they can see your video. However, it is a double edged sword; if you have derogatory content on youtube it could hurt your recruiting prospects. **Facebook** can be a useful social networking site where you can join pages from different schools and start networking with current students, coaches, alumni, and staff. However, it can also hurt you if there is disparaging content on your Face book page in the form of pictures, videos and/or written content. Use these sites to build a positive image of yourself.

Finding College & Coach Information

College Coaches Online *www.collegecoachesonline.com* is the best source I could find that you can use to find colleges by division, geography, association, etc. This is a fee based service whereas you can buy a CD Rom or purchase an on-line subscription by the month or year.

Contact with Coaches

As it is with most conversations between minors and adults who are trying to sell something, they should be managed. Student-athletes should be prepared to direct the direction of the conversation to reduce the opportunity for coaches to sell student-athletes on their product; the university, their program or promises. Parents should regulate the phone conversations to days of the week and times. This information should be provided to coaches on questionnaires and introductory letters. Phone conversations can be a waste of time if they are not managed properly. Following are some questions that student-athletes and/or parents/guardians can ask to insure colleges are serious about recruiting a student.

1. Are you interested in signing a letter of intent during the early signing period?

This question helps to uncover where the coaches rate you on the depth chart of potential athletes. You may receive varying responses that basically says, "We are not ready to sign you until we know what players we have ranked higher than you says about playing for us". What this provides is the truth of where you stand with this school and coach. This is why it is so important to start recruiting early.

2. Do you plan on making a home visit?

This is not an elimination question, but it is a question that will provide you with some information on where you stand with the coach. If you receive a yes, schedule it on a calendar, palm pilot or electronic calendar and prepare to meet with them. If they say no, listen to hear whether they have already made offers to other players and where you sit on their priority list. Be patient and polite because they may want to visit right before or during the signing period.

3. When can we expect an invitation for an official visit?

Usually a school that pays for an official visit is a school that is interested in you in a big way. Rules allow schools to offer only so many official visits and if you are one of them, that is a good thing. If they do not offer an official visit, the school may not have evaluated your film or will be looking forward to seeing you play again in person.

These are the top three questions to determine if you are high on a coaches priority list, primarily because all of these questions deal with money, budgets and restrictions. If a coach is willing to sign you early, make a home visit, or pay for an official visit, they are serious.

4. Ask the coaches what they have seen in your film or play that has impressed them?

This will determine whether or not they have evaluated you and ranked you in their depth chart. Coaches make calls as a result of information they have received from recruiting services, as a result of camps or combines you have attended, and want to find out where you stand in the recruiting process as well as how much interest there is for you.

Negotiation Tactics of College Coaches

There are those times when student-athletes are so focused at playing at a big name school even though they have the ability to play at a smaller school that the coach decides that they could expand their pool of athletes by requesting the student-athlete **Walk-on.** A walk-on is a tryout. There is no obligation by the coach to provide a roster spot, but the player is not discouraged to tryout. Walk on practices when school starts and there are no promises of a scholarship. The movie Rudy was really successful at showing how a walk on with minimal ability ended up playing a few downs in an actual game for Notre Dame.

The **Preferred walk on** is a term coined by coaches to sell a student-athlete into walking on to their program with a non-scholarship, but highly recommended status. It comes sometimes with the caveat that you will get an extra look for trying on to a team. This is usually again as the result of a student-athlete who wants to play at a big name school or at a level higher than where he/she would actually get playing time. The preferred walk-on however, is a great sales approach by a coach to build his roster with able bodies to compete and practice. These student-athletes can start practicing with the team and report with the returning players and incoming freshman. In either case as a walk-on or preferred walk-on there is no commitment by the coach or the staff and it should say to you that they believe very little in your ability to contribute at their school. Furthermore, they are not willing to commit any financial scholarship aid to show their commitment. This is why waiting and not being involved with enough schools can be a limiting factor at reducing your ability to be awarded an athletic scholarship. **Partial scholarship** is the norm in Division II, NAIA, and non-revenue sports because the smaller division schools sometimes have fewer scholarships to offer, however, they want to build their teams and programs with as many players as they can to develop and compete in practice. Many smaller division schools give very few full scholarships. These are often given to transferring athletes from high divisions. Also division I non-revenue sports often build their rosters on partial scholarships. It does not mean you cannot earn a full scholarship with your play or be in the position to negotiate with a coach who offers the aforementioned options. You can be in a position to negotiate by being in contact with more schools and have other options on the table, leveraging those options against the school that makes these offers.

Recruiting Visits

There are three types of recruiting visits that student-athletes can experience during the recruiting process. The **Unofficial Visit** is one of the most important. It involves scheduling visits to colleges to view their campus and learn what they have to offer in terms of education and what their institution does best for its students. These visits are completely informal and very useful to get a realistic view of private versus public type institutions, facilities, geographic locations, doctrine and non-religious schools. Unofficial visits also come in terms of tickets to junior days for student-athletes and tickets to the college's athletic events. Often times during junior days, players get a glimpse into the college's athletic and academic programs. This is one reason why it is important to get started early in the recruiting process and have the opportunity to experience as many schools as possible. **Official Visits** are usually a signal from a coach that you are high on their priority list as a student-athlete because these are paid visits by the coaching staff that often involve overnight stays. By NCAA rules, student-athletes can experience five official visits their senior year. This is usually a great opportunity to meet the players on the team and the entire coaching staff.

Home visits are also another indication that you are high on a school's recruiting list. This is when a coach visits your home, meets your family, and delivers a written letter of intent.

Right School Decision

Finding the right school whether you are a student-athlete or not, comes down to what your family can afford to pay and how much debt you are willing to take on to attend a school in the end. However, other factors that contribute are location, size, major offerings, facilities, coaches, professors, and much more. I love watching the Army All American All Star football game and watching all the elite blue chip athletes pull their hats out of a bag to announce the school they have chosen to attend out of 5-10 schools. The reality for the other 99% of us is that we hope a college coach chooses us and gives us a hat to wear, bearing the college's name. As a football coach and recruiting specialist, I often listen to parents and grandparents speak for their young student-athletes and communicate that they want their son or daughter to be close to home so that they can drive to see them. It is highly suggested that student-athletes take into account the number of schools that are a couple of states away that are offer forms of scholarship aid (athletic, academic & grants). The ultimate decision should always be left in the hands of the student-athlete in consideration of how much aid has been offered to cover the cost of attendance. No school that is offering aid should be discounted until analysis and research has been performed.

College Planning Resources

Personal Pre-College Assessment:
The following survey can be useful in rating colleges you research versus the right fit for you academically, geographically, emotionally and athletically. Start this process early!

<u>5</u> is perfect for me, <u>4</u> is close to what I want, <u>3</u> is an ok fit, <u>2</u> is probably not, <u>1</u> is just wrong

Institution Name: _____

1. **Rate the college admission academic requirements**
   High   Moderate   Average   Low
2. **Colleges curriculum offering versus what you want to study**
   Exact   Close   Moderate   None
3. **Distance to my home town?**
   1-3 Hrs   4-7 Hrs   8-11 Hrs
4. **Schools geographic location**
   Rural   Urban
5. **The size of the school**
   <3,500   >3,500   >10,000   >20,000
6. **The schools religious affiliation**
   Christian   Non-denominational   Catholic   Other
7. **The faculty to student ratio**
   3-8 to 1   9-14 to 1   17-22 to 1
8. **Graduation rate for incoming freshman?**
   20%   40%   60%   80%
9. **Graduation rate for student-athletes?**
   40%   60%   80%   100%
10. **Campus facilities for student-athletes and academic development?**
    Leading State of the Art   Current   Out dated

Rank College from one to ten 1 = Perfect - 10 = Not a chance _____
Colleges that rank high on your list should be contacted. Request information from the college athletic department to become part of their recruiting pool. I suggest beginning this process during your freshman and sophomore year and perform this for a minimum of 150 colleges.

The following recruiting matrix is also useful for tracking schools that contact you with questionnaires or requests for film, transcripts and/or letters of recommendations.

College Recruiting Call Matrix for Student-Athletes					
Athlete's Name: _____					
Class:					
Name of School	Recruiting Coach	Phone Number	Division	Coaches Request	Completed
1.					
2.					
3.					
4.					
5.					
Pertinent Questions to ask coaches if you speak with them					

Will you be offering an official visit?

Will you be visiting me and my family for a home visit?

How many other athletes are you recruiting at my position?

Where do I stand on your depth sheet?

Cost of Attendance Calculations				
	College #1	*College #2*	*College #3*	*College #4*
College Name	**Example College**			
Amount Athletic Scholarship	$ -			
Amount of Academic Scholarship #1	$ 15,000.00			
Amount Of Academic Scholarship #2	$ 8,000.00			
Amount of Grants (Federal Aid)	$ 6,500.00			
Total Financial Aid Award	**$ 29,500.00**	$ -	$ -	$ -
Cost of Tuition	$ (34,950.00)			
Cost of Room & Board	$ (8,950.00)			
est. Cost of Books & Supplies	$ (900.00)			
Estimated Miscellaneous Expenses	$ (700.00)			
Total Cost of Attendance	**$ (45,500.00)**	$ -	$ -	$ -
"Out of Pocket" Costs per year	**$ (16,000.00)**	$ -	$ -	$ -

Post-College Visit Survey

Take a moment to complete this post college visit survey to measure your compatibility with the university after an "official visit".

University Name_____

1. The coaches & players made me feel welcome to the university
   Yes   No
2. I felt like their curriculum, staff and support facilities will support my career aspirations
   Yes   No
3. What scholarship package was offered?
   Athletic   Academic   Full   Partial
4. What is the possibility of me playing for this program?
   High   Medium   Low
5. I liked the combination of size & location of the school
   Yes   No
6. During the visit, the coaches made an effort to discuss my non-sport career aspiration
   Yes   No
7. The coaches & players seemed to authentically care about each other
   Yes   No
8. Players on the team spoke with enthusiasm about the prospects of their non-sport career after college
   Yes   No

What is the best type of recruiting company to use?

How many college coaches know your name and what you bring to the table athletically and academically? One way to go from high school to college and participate in a collegiate sport is to have a college coach or recruiter evaluate you. If you are not rated in all the top magazines as one of the top 150-200 players in your sport, how does a college evaluate your potential? When I played, I saw athletes get recruited to Division I colleges and some players who I thought were just as good did not get recruited at all. Once I got into coaching after college, I learned one of the reasons had to do with grades; another is EXPOSURE. There are recruiting services that provide colleges with pools of athletes based on the need of the colleges. These services are paid for by the colleges to compile a list of qualified recruiting prospects. The purpose of finding a recruiting company to serve a non-blue chip athlete is to provide student-athletes with the exposure & education they need to be evaluated by colleges and create an opportunity to be one of the beneficiaries of the **1 Billion Dollars in college aid that is rewarded per year to more than 126,000 student-athletes ~ according to the National Collegiate Athletic Association (NCAA).** For those of you who don't know, college aid encompasses athletic and academic scholarships. I have researched online, read articles and books on these companies, and it seems that many of these businesses are preying on the emotions of parents and student-athletes and in the end the parents are not getting what they paid for. These companies have elaborate web-sites and slogans and many charge between $700-$3000 dollars for their services. My evocation is that if they are not providing athletic training to your son/daughter for those prices, I would suggest you research them before paying $1000's of dollars for a promise of athletic scholarship that no recruiting service can guarantee. Families have gone bankrupt in an attempt to provide their sons/daughters with the opportunity to be successful at the next level. A recruiting firm should provide a great deal of education to the student-athlete and their parents, complete with a system designed for parents who have the time to do themselves. College coaches contact information is PUBLIC information and is sold on discs for $29.95—see *www.collegecaochesonline.com.* Therefore, if you have the time, the best recruiting company is one that provides you and the high school with the recruiting resources, a system and educational model on the process to assist them in building a recruiting program for the youth of that community. Honestly, very few recruiting companies provide a comprehensive recruiting package that completely restructures and streamlines the process into a cost & time effective approach that offer student-athletes the opportunity to be awarded an athletic scholarship. A good recruiting education company will assist you in the following:

- ✓ Develop athletic résumé's
- ✓ Develop promotional letters
- ✓ Be available to educate you on the process
- ✓ Provide their educational model to high school coaches
- ✓ Provide Full Student-athlete evaluations (academic & athletic)

Moreover, a recruiting company that does not provide a comprehensive program for the athletic department at your school, student-athletes and parents should at the least provide you with some type of preparatory service to build athletic resumes and introductory letters to send to colleges. Furthermore they should provide you the service of submitting that information to every college on an annual, bi-annual or quarterly basis to update coaches on your progress and what you are doing in the off-season and how you have improved statistically and measurably from season to season. Their educational system should also reach the needs of coaches who often don't have the time to do the recruiting process. The following company provides all of the above.

- ✓ Recruiting education seminars, training & services: *www.noblesteps.com*

Division I Eligibility Requirements
(Estimated 326 - DI=117, DIAA=121, DIAAA=88)

Your classification as a student-athlete upon entering college will be a "Qualifier" or "Partial Qualifier"

- ✓ **Qualifiers** means all the requirements (ACT/SAT/GPA) and can play as a true freshman and receive an athletic scholarship
- ✓ **Partial Qualifiers** means you cannot play as a freshman but can practice and receive an athletic scholarship if you receive a bachelor's degree before your 5th year. You will have four years of eligibility; if not you will only receive three years
- ✓ A Division I Qualifier Requirements
- ✓ Graduate high school
- ✓ Graduate with a core-course GPA/Total SAT/ACT scores per the Qualifier Index
- ✓ Pass core curriculum of at least 13 academic course units

Division I Qualifier Index		
Core GPA	Total ACT	SAT
2.5 and up	68	820
2.475	70	830
2.450	70	840-850
2.425	70	860
2.400	71	860
2.375	72	870
2.350	73	880
2.325	74	890
2.300	75	900
2.275	76	910
2.250	77	920
2.225	78	930
2.200	79	940
2.175	80	950
2.150	80	960
2.125	81	960
2.100	82	970
2.075	83	980
2.050	84	990
2.025	85	1000
2.000	86	1010

Division I Academic Qualifiers Requirements
English—4 Years
Math (Algebra1 or Higher) 3 years
Sciences (Natural or Physical)—2 Years
Additional English, math or Science—1 year
Social Sciences—2 Years
4 years of Additional Courses (foreign Language, non doctrinal religion, philosophy)

Division I member institutions have to sponsor at the minimum seven men and seven men sports. For schools with division I football are classified as Football Bowl Division (division 1-A) and NCAA Championship Subdivision is (division 1-AA). Football Bowl Subdivision teams have to meet a minimum requirement 15,000 in attendance, however the Championship Bowl Subdivision schools do not have to meet the minimum attendance.

Division II Eligibility Requirements
(Estimated 219 Institutions)

Your classification as a student-athlete upon entering college will be a "Qualifier" or "Partial Qualifier"

- ✓ **Qualifiers** means all the requirements (ACT/SAT/GPA) and can play as a true freshman and receive an athletic scholarship.
- ✓ **Partial Qualifiers** means you cannot play as a freshman but can practice and receive an athletic scholarship; you will have four years of eligibility.
- ✓ Graduate High school.
- ✓ Graduate with a 2.0 core course GPA.
- ✓ Score a minimum combined SAT score.
- ✓ Complete core curriculum of at least 13 academic courses.

Division II Academic Qualifiers Requirements
English—3 Years
Math (Algebra1 or Higher)—2 years
Science (Physical or Natural) & lab science—2 Years
Additional English, math or Science—2 year
Social Sciences—2 Years
3 years of Additional Courses (foreign Language, non doctrinal religion, philosophy)

- ✓ No sliding scale.

Division II sports programs have to sponsor five men and five women sports and two team sports for each gender. Most Division II athletes play their sport with a combination of athletic scholarships, grants, student loans, academic scholarships, and work study program earnings.

NCAA Division III Requirements
(Estimated 419 Institutions)

Do not offer scholarships but are immensely prominent when it comes to academics. They can offer substantial academic scholarships to assist in covering the cost of attendance.

✓ They do not have standards requirements
✓ Each school is different (Ask)

Division III schools have to sponsor five women and five women sports. At division III schools academics are more of a focus with the sports not being a year round commitment. DIII schools do offer grants and financial aid packages that can match DI and DII athletic scholarships. Division III school programs are built around student-athletes and the impact of sports.

NAIA Eligibility Requirements (Estimated 288 Institutions)

An estimated 90% of NAIA schools offer athletic scholarships with roughly 50,000 student-athletes participating in nearly 300 institutions in the United States and Canada. They have 25 conferences that play for championships in 13 sports. These schools are similar to division III schools where programs focus on the total student-athlete experience. Learn more about this division at *http://naia.cstv.com/*

✓ Graduate in the upper half of your high school class
✓ Earn a minimum combined ACT/SAT score
✓ Earn a 2.0 cumulative

NJCAA Academic Requirements (Estimated 503 Institutions)

NJCAA schools are a great choice for student-athletes that do not have the grades to be admitted into a NCAA Division I, II or III institution. They offer 15 sports at over 300 2-year colleges. Division I and II NJCAA schools focus on different sports in 43 states in the US. Only division I and II JUCO schools offer athletic scholarships. JUCO schools are historically and continue to be a hotbed for Division I and II colleges to recruit. Learn more about JUCO schools at: *www.njcaa.org/*

✓ Graduate from high school
✓ Receive the equivalency diploma
✓ Pass a GED

NCAA, NAIA & NJCAA Sports Offerings

There are more sports offering scholarships than we are accustomed to knowing. The following will provide you with a glimpse into emerging and equivalent sports. Emerging sports according to the NCAA are intended to provide new opportunities to female student-athletes. Find a sport below and check into the link to learn more about how you can compete in the sport. Equivalency Sports are available and offer partial and full ride scholarships.

Archery—NCAA	Gymnastics—NCAA
US Collegiate Archery	College Gymnastics
www.uscollegiatearchery.org/	*www.collegegymnastics.org*
NCAA Institutions Sponsoring (Women)—1	NCAA Institutions Sponsoring (Men)—18
Badminton—NCAA	**Rifle—NCAA**
Intercollegiate Badminton	College Rifle Coaches
www.ibabadminton.com/	*www.collegerifle.com*
NCAA Institutions Sponsoring (Women)—2	NCAA Institutions (Women)—11
Bowling—NCAA	NCAA Institutions (Men)—4
College Bowling	NCAA Institutions (Mixed)—25
www.collegebowling.com	**Skiing—NCAA**
NCAA Institutions Sponsoring (Women)—56	US Collegiate Ski & Snowboard Association
NCAA Institutions Sponsoring (Men)—2	*www.uscsa.com*
Equestrian—NCAA	NCAA Institutions Sponsoring (Women)—40
The College Equestrian	NCAA Institutions Sponsoring (Men)—37
www.thecollegeequestrian.com	**Rugby—NCAA**
NCAA Institutions Sponsoring (Women)—38	USA College Rugby
NCAA Institutions Sponsoring (Men) 10	*www.usacollegerugby.com*
Fencing—NCAA	NCAA Institutions Sponsoring (Women)—
College Fencing 360	**Squash—NCAA**
www.collegefencing360.com	College Squash Association
NCAA Institutions Sponsoring (Women)—42	*www.squashtalk.com*
NCAA Institutions Sponsoring (Men)—33	NCAA Institutions Sponsoring (Women)—28
	Synchronized Swimming—NCAA
	United States Synchronized Swimming
	www.usasynchro.org
	NCAA Institutions Sponsoring (Women)—8

Recruiting Opportunities & Evaluation Standards—
Baseball
10.9% from High School to College

Collegiate Baseball NCAA Division I		Baseball Websites
Number of Schools Offering Baseball	291	
Athletic Scholarships per School	11.7	*www.abca.org* *www.hsbaseballweb.com* *www.aaronslink.com* *www.baseball-links.com* *www.heavyhitter.com* *www.thebaseballportal.com*
NCAA Division II		
Number of Schools Offering Baseball	242	
Athletic Scholarships per School	9	
NCAA Division III		
Number of Schools Offering Baseball	373	**Evaluation Standards**
Academic, Need, Merit, Grants. etc.	all	
NAIA		Speed: Home to First 60 Yard Dash Arm Strength Home to second Pop Time Pitches: Fastball, curve, Chang-up, etc
Number of Schools Offering Baseball	213	
Athletic Scholarships per School	12	
NJCAA		
Number of Schools Offering Baseball	397	
Athletic Scholarships per School	n/a	

Recruiting Opportunities & Evaluation Standards—
Men's Basketball
5.1% from High School to College

Collegiate Men's Basketball Opportunities NCAA Division I		Basketball Websites
Number of Schools Offering Men's Basketball	333	*www.thebasketballportal.com* *www.basketball-toplinks.com*
Athletic Scholarships per School	13	*www.collegehoopsnet.com* *www.rivalshoops.com*
NCAA Division II		*www.hoopsmaster.com* *www.D3hoops.com*
Number of Schools Offering Men's Basketball	288	
Athletic Scholarships per School	10	**Evaluation Standards**
NCAA Division III		
Number of Schools Offering Men's Basketball	412	Post Skills Rebounding Skills
Academic, Need, Merit, Grants. Etc.	all	Shot Blocking Outside Shooting Range
NAIA		Court Speed
Number of Schools Offering Men's Basketball	261	Penetration Ability Court Awareness
Athletic Scholarships per School-Div I	11	Ball Handling Skills
Athletic Scholarships per School-Div-II	6	Passing Ability
NJCAA		
Number of Schools Offering Men's Basketball	436	
Athletic Scholarships per School	n/a	

Recruiting Opportunities & Evaluation Standards— Women's Basketball
5.3% from High School to College

Collegiate Women's Basketball Opportunities		Basketball Websites
NCAA Division I		*www.thebasketballportal.com*
Number of Schools Offering Women's Basketball	331	*www.basketball-toplinks.com*
Athletic Scholarships per School	15	*www.wbca.org* *www.collegehoopsnet.com*
NCAA Division II		*www.rivalshoops.com* *www.hoopsmaster.com*
Number of Schools Offering Women's Basketball	289	*www.D3hoops.com*
Athletic Scholarships per School	10	**Evaluation Standards**
NCAA Division III		
Number of Schools Offering Women's Basketball	436	Post Skills
Academic, Need, Merit, Grants. etc.	all	Rebounding Skills Shot Blocking
NAIA		Outside Shooting Range
Number of Schools Offering Women's Basketball	260	Court Speed Penetration Ability
Athletic Scholarships per School-Div I	11	Court Awareness
Athletic Scholarships per School-Div-II	6	Ball Handling Skills Passing Ability
NJCAA		
Number of Schools Offering Women's Basketball	396	
Athletic Scholarships per School	n/a	

Recruiting Opportunities & Evaluation Standards— Men's Crew

Collegiate Men's Crew Opportunities NCAA Division I	
Number of Schools Offering Men's Crew	28
Athletic Scholarships per School	0
NCAA Division II	
Number of Schools Offering Men's Crew	4
Athletic Scholarships per School	0
NCAA Division III	
Number of Schools Offering Men's Crew	31
Academic, Need, Merit, Grants. etc.	all

Evaluation Standard is based on Heavy/Lightweight— Upper/Lower Level times

Recruiting Opportunities & Evaluation Standards— Women's Crew

Collegiate Women's Crew Opportunities NCAA Division I	
Number of Schools Offering Women's Crew	86
Athletic Scholarships per School	20
NCAA Division II	
Number of Schools Offering Women's Crew	16
Athletic Scholarships per School	20
NCAA Division III	
Number of Schools Offering Women's Crew	43
Academic, Need, Merit, Grants. etc.	All

Evaluation Standard is based on Heavy/Lightweight— Upper/Lower Level times

Recruiting Opportunities & Evaluation Standards—
Men's Cross Country
8.4% from High School to College

Collegiate Cross Country Opportunities NCAA Division I		Cross Country Websites Cross Country Related Links
Number of Schools Offering Men's Cross Country	301	
Athletic Scholarships per School	12.6	*www.uscca.org* *www.dyestat.com* *www.track-and-field.net* *www.tflinks.com*
NCAA Division II		
Number of Schools Offering Men's Cross Country	241	
Athletic Scholarships per School	12.6	**Evaluation Standards**
NCAA Division III		
Number of Schools Offering Men's Cross Country	372	1/2 Mile Time 1 Mile Time
Academic, Need, Merit, Grants. etc.	all	2 Mile Time 3.1 Mile Time
NAIA		
Number of Schools Offering Men's Cross Country	204	
Athletic Scholarships per School-Div I	5	
NJCAA		
Number of Schools Offering Men's Cross Country	114	
Athletic Scholarships per School	n/a	

Recruiting Opportunities & Evaluation Standards—
Women's Cross Country
10.9% from High School to College

Collegiate Cross Country Opportunities NCAA Division I		Cross Country Websites Cross Country Related Links www.usccca.org www.dyestat.com www.track-and-field.net www.tflinks.com
Number of Schools Offering Women's Cross Country	327	
Athletic Scholarships per School	18	
NCAA Division II		
Number of Schools Offering Women's Cross Country	270	
Athletic Scholarships per School	12.6	**Evaluation Standards**
NCAA Division III		
Number of Schools Offering Women's Cross Country	393	1/2 Mile Time
Academic, Need, Merit, Grants. etc.	All	1 Mile Time 2 Mile Time
NAIA		3.1 Mile Time
Number of Schools Offering Women's Cross Country	211	
Athletic Scholarships per School-Div I	5	
NJCAA		
Number of Schools Offering Women's Cross Country	123	
Athletic Scholarships per School	n/a	

Recruiting Opportunities & Evaluation Standards—
Field Hockey
9.9% from High School to College

Collegiate Field Hockey Opportunities NCAA Division I		Field Hockey Websites Field Hockey Related Links
Number of Schools Offering Field Hockey	77	*www.nfhca.org*
Athletic Scholarships per School	12	*www.usfieldhockey.com*
NCAA Division II		*www.hockeylinx.com* *www.planetfieldhockey.com*
Number of Schools Offering Field Hockey	26	
Athletic Scholarships per School	6.3	**Evaluation Standards**
NCAA Division III		Speed—40 yard dash
Number of Schools Offering Field Hockey	158	Balance Agility
Academic, Need, Merit, Grants etc.	all	Vision Passing ability
NAIA		Hitting Trapping and tackling
Number of Schools Offering Field Hockey	3	Carrying the ball Dribbling
Athletic Scholarships per School-Div I	n/a	Positioning in attack Covering
NJCAA		Defending
Number of Schools Offering Field Hockey	10	
Athletic Scholarships per School	n/a	

Recruiting Opportunities & Evaluation Standards— Football
7.6% from High School to College

Collegiate Football Opportunities NCAA Division I		Football Websites Football Related Links
Number of Schools Offering Football	119	*www.afca.org*
Athletic Scholarships per School	85	*www.ncaafootball.com*
NCAA Division 1-AA		*www.rivals.com*
		www.scout.com
Number of Schools Offering Football	119	
Athletic Scholarships per School	63	**Evaluation Standards**
NCAA Division II		
Number of Schools Offering Football	154	Field Speed
		40 Yard Dash
Athletic Scholarships per School	36	20 Yard Shuttle
NCAA Division III		Vertical Jump
		Broad Jump
Number of Schools Offering Football	239	3 Cone Drill
Academic, Need, Merit, Grants etc.	all	Blocking
NAIA		Tackling
		Catching
Number of Schools Offering Football	3	Arm Strength
Athletic Scholarships per School-Div I	24	Physical Strength
NJCAA		
Number of Schools Offering Football	70	
Athletic Scholarships per School	n/a	

Recruiting Opportunities & Evaluation Standards—
Men's Golf
7.6% from High School to College

Collegiate Men's Golf Opportunities NCAA Division I		Golf Websites Men's Golf Related Links
Number of Schools Offering Men's Golf	291	
Athletic Scholarships per School	4.5	*www.ngca.com*
NCAA Division II		*www.cgfgolf.org* *www.nagce.org*
Number of Schools Offering Men's Golf	210	
Athletic Scholarships per School	3.6	**Evaluation Standards**
NCAA Division III		
Number of Schools Offering Men's Golf	284	Score versus Par
Academic, Need, Merit, Grants etc.	all	
NAIA		
Number of Schools Offering Men's Golf	184	
Athletic Scholarships per School-Div I	5	
NJCAA		
Number of Schools Offering Men's Golf	216	
Athletic Scholarships per School	n/a	

Recruiting Opportunities & Evaluation Standards—
Women's Golf
9.7% from High School to College

Collegiate Women's Golf Opportunities NCAA Division I		Golf Websites Women's Golf Related Links
Number of Schools Offering Women's Golf	243	*www.ngca.com*
Athletic Scholarships per School	6	*www.cgfgolf.org*
NCAA Division II		*www.nagce.org*
Number of Schools Offering Women's Golf	134	**Evaluation Standards**
Athletic Scholarships per School	5.4	
NCAA Division III		Score versus Par
Number of Schools Offering Women's Golf	164	
Academic, Need, Merit, Grants etc.	all	
NAIA		
Number of Schools Offering Women's Golf	145	
Athletic Scholarships per School-Div I	5	
NJCAA		
Number of Schools Offering Women's Golf	88	
Athletic Scholarships per School	n/a	

Recruiting Opportunities & Evaluation Standards—
Women's Gymnastics
7.0% from High School to College

Collegiate Women's Gymnastics Opportunities	
NCAA Division I	
Number of Schools Offering Women's Gymnastics	63
Athletic Scholarships per School	10
NCAA Division II	
Number of Schools Offering Women's Gymnastics	5
Athletic Scholarships per School	6
NCAA Division III	
Number of Schools Offering Women's Gymnastics	16
Academic, Need, Merit, Grants etc.	all

Recruiting Opportunities & Evaluation Standards—
Men's Hockey
13.5% from High School to College

Collegiate Men's Hockey Opportunities NCAA Division I		Hockey Websites
Number of Schools Offering Men's Hockey	58	*www.ahcahockey.com* *www.collegehockey.org* *www.azhockey.com* *www.uscollegehockey.com*
Athletic Scholarships per School	18	
NCAA Division II		
Number of Schools Offering Men's Hockey	7	
Athletic Scholarships per School	18	
NCAA Division III		
Number of Schools Offering Men's Hockey	73	
Academic, Need, Merit, Grants etc.	all	
NAIA		
Number of Schools Offering Men's Hockey	7	
Athletic Scholarships per School-Div I	n/a	
NJCAA		
Number of Schools Offering Men's Hockey	10	
Athletic Scholarships per School	n/a	

Recruiting Opportunities & Evaluation Standards—
Women's Hockey
32.6% from High School to College

Collegiate Women's Hockey Opportunities NCAA Division I		Hockey Websites
Number of Schools Offering Women's Hockey	35	*www.ahcahockey.com* *www.collegehockey.org* *www.azhockey.com* *www.uscollegehockey.com*
Athletic Scholarships per School	18	
NCAA Division II		
Number of Schools Offering Women's Hockey	2	
Athletic Scholarships per School	18	
NCAA Division III		
Number of Schools Offering Women's Hockey	46	
Academic, Need, Merit, Grants etc.	all	
NAIA		
Number of Schools Offering Women's Hockey	7	
Athletic Scholarships per School-Div I	n/a	
NJCAA		
Number of Schools Offering Women's Hockey	10	
Athletic Scholarships per School	n/a	

Recruiting Opportunities & Evaluation Standards—
Men's Lacrosse
22.7% from High School to College

Collegiate Men's Lacrosse Opportunities NCAA Division I		Lacrosse Websites
Number of Schools Offering Men's Lacrosse	57	*www.lacrosse.org*
Athletic Scholarships per School	12.6	*www.iwlca.org*
NCAA Division II		*www.insidelacrosse.com*
Number of Schools Offering Men's Lacrosse	35	*www.laxtips.com*
Athletic Scholarships per School	10.8	**Evaluation Standards**
NCAA Division III		Scoring ability
Number of Schools Offering Men's Lacrosse	151	Vision
Academic, Need, Merit, Grants etc.	all	Passing ability
NAIA		Size
Number of Schools Offering Men's Lacrosse	5	Speed
Athletic Scholarships per School-Div I	n/a	Checking ability
NJCAA		Stick skills
Number of Schools Offering Men's Lacrosse	27	Body positioning
Athletic Scholarships per School	n/a	Arc & Angle play

Recruiting Opportunities & Evaluation Standards—
Women's Lacrosse
21.0% from High School to College

Collegiate Women's Lacrosse Opportunities NCAA Division I		Lacrosse Websites
Number of Schools Offering Women's Lacrosse	85	*www.lacrosse.org* *www.iwlca.org* *www.insidelacrosse.com* *www.laxtips.com*
Athletic Scholarships per School	12	
NCAA Division II		
Number of Schools Offering Women's Lacrosse	48	**Evaluation Standards**
Athletic Scholarships per School	9.9	
NCAA Division III		Scoring ability
Number of Schools Offering Women's Lacrosse	180	Vision Passing ability Size
Academic, Need, Merit, Grants etc.	all	Speed
NAIA		Checking ability Stick skills
Number of Schools Offering Women's Lacrosse	3	Body positioning Arc & Angle play
Athletic Scholarships per School-Div I	n/a	
NJCAA		
Number of Schools Offering Women's Lacrosse	16	
Athletic Scholarships per School	n/a	

Recruiting Opportunities & Evaluation Standards— Men's Soccer
9.5% from High School to College

Collegiate Men's Soccer Opportunities NCAA Division I		Soccer Websites
Number of Schools Offering Men's Soccer	198	*www.nscaa.com* *www.soccer-corner.com* *www.soccerinfo.com*
Athletic Scholarships per School	9.9	
NCAA Division II		
Number of Schools Offering Men's Soccer	179	
Athletic Scholarships per School	9	
NCAA Division III		
Number of Schools Offering Men's Soccer	401	
Academic, Need, Merit, Grants etc.	all	
NAIA		
Number of Schools Offering Men's Soccer	218	
Athletic Scholarships per School-Div I	12	
NJCAA		
Number of Schools Offering Men's Soccer	220	
Athletic Scholarships per School	n/a	

Recruiting Opportunities & Evaluation Standards—
Women's Soccer
10.9% from High School to College

Collegiate Women's Soccer Opportunities NCAA Division I		Soccer Websites
Number of Schools Offering Women's Soccer	310	*www.nscaa.com* *www.soccer-corner.com* *www.soccerinfo.com*
Athletic Scholarships per School	11	
NCAA Division II		
Number of Schools Offering Women's Soccer	225	
Athletic Scholarships per School	9.9	
NCAA Division III		
Number of Schools Offering Women's Soccer	424	
Academic, Need, Merit, Grants etc.	all	
NAIA		
Number of Schools Offering Women's Soccer	219	
Athletic Scholarships per School-Div I	12	
NJCAA		
Number of Schools Offering Women's Soccer	183	
Athletic Scholarships per School	n/a	

Recruiting Opportunities & Evaluation Standards—
Softball
7.8% from High School to College

Collegiate Softball Opportunities NCAA Division I		Softball Websites
Number of Schools Offering Softball	276	*www.nfcaa.org*
Athletic Scholarships per School	12	*www.softballtournaments.com*
NCAA Division II		*www.playnsa.com*
Number of Schools Offering Softball	268	*www.softball.org*
Athletic Scholarships per School	7.2	**Evaluation Standards**
NCAA Division III		
Number of Schools Offering Softball	408	Home to First Speed
Academic, Need, Merit, Grants etc.	all	Home to Home Speed
NAIA		Arm Strength
Number of Schools Offering Softball	212	
Athletic Scholarships per School-Div I	10	
NJCAA		
Number of Schools Offering Softball	360	
Athletic Scholarships per School	n/a	

Recruiting Opportunities & Evaluation Standards—
Men's Swimming
9.9% from High School to College

Collegiate Men's Swimming Opportunities NCAA Division I		Swimming Websites
Number of Schools Offering Men's Swimming	139	*www.swimmingcoach.org*
Athletic Scholarships per School	9.9	*www.cscaa.org* *www.nisca.net* *www.swimnews.com*
NCAA Division II		
Number of Schools Offering Men's Swimming	56	**Evaluation Standards**
Athletic Scholarships per School	8.1	Event Times
NCAA Division III		
Number of Schools Offering Men's Swimming	197	
Academic, Need, Merit, Grants etc.	all	
NAIA		
Number of Schools Offering Men's Swimming	23	
Athletic Scholarships per School-Div I	8	
NJCAA		
Number of Schools Offering Men's Swimming	18	
Athletic Scholarships per School	n/a	

Recruiting Opportunities & Evaluation Standards—
Women's Swimming
8.5% from High School to College

Collegiate Women's Swimming Opportunities NCAA Division I		Swimming Websites
Number of Schools Offering Women's Swimming	193	*www.swimmingcoach.org*
Athletic Scholarships per School	14	*www.cscaa.org* *www.nisca.net* *www.swimnews.com*
NCAA Division II		
Number of Schools Offering Women's Swimming	72	**Evaluation Standards**
Athletic Scholarships per School	8.1	Event Times
NCAA Division III		
Number of Schools Offering Women's Swimming	242	
Academic, Need, Merit, Grants etc.	all	
NAIA		
Number of Schools Offering Women's Swimming	32	
Athletic Scholarships per School-Div I	8	
NJCAA		
Number of Schools Offering Women's Swimming	18	
Athletic Scholarships per School	n/a	

Recruiting Opportunities & Evaluation Standards—
Men's Tennis
6.6% from High School to College

Collegiate Men's Tennis Opportunities NCAA Division I		Tennis Websites
Number of Schools Offering Men's Tennis	258	*www.ushsta.org* *www.collegetennisonline.com* *www.collegeandjunior* *tennis.com* *www.itatennis.com* *www.tennisserver.com* *www.tennis4all.com*
Athletic Scholarships per School	4.5	
NCAA Division II		
Number of Schools Offering Men's Tennis	168	
Athletic Scholarships per School	4.5	
NCAA Division III		
Number of Schools Offering Men's Tennis	325	
Academic, Need, Merit, Grants etc.	all	
NAIA		
Number of Schools Offering Men's Tennis	106	
Athletic Scholarships per School-Div I	5	
NJCAA		
Number of Schools Offering Men's Tennis	80	
Athletic Scholarships per School	n/a	

Recruiting Opportunities & Evaluation Standards—
Women's Tennis
8.1% from High School to College

Collegiate Women's Tennis Opportunities NCAA Division I		Tennis Websites
Number of Schools Offering Women's Tennis	311	*www.ushsta.org* *www.collegetennisonline.com* *www.collegeandjunior tennis.com* *www.itatennis.com* *www.tennisserver.com* *www.tennis4all.com*
Athletic Scholarships per School	8	
NCAA Division II		
Number of Schools Offering Women's Tennis	220	
Athletic Scholarships per School	6	
NCAA Division III		
Number of Schools Offering Women's Tennis	371	
Academic, Need, Merit, Grants etc.	all	
NAIA		
Number of Schools Offering Women's Tennis	123	
Athletic Scholarships per School-Div I	5	
NJCAA		
Number of Schools Offering Women's Tennis	95	
Athletic Scholarships per School	n/a	

Recruiting Opportunities & Evaluation Standards—
Men's Track
7.5% from High School to College

Collegiate Men's Track & Field Opportunities		Track Websites
NCAA Division I		www.dyestat.com
Number of Schools Offering Men's Track & Field	269	www.track-and-field.net
Athletic Scholarships per School	12.6	www.usatf.org www.trackinfo.org
NCAA Division II		
Number of Schools Offering Men's Track & Field	162	**Evaluation Standard**
Athletic Scholarships per School	12.6	Event Times &
NCAA Division III		Measurements
Number of Schools Offering Men's Track & Field	267	
Academic, Need, Merit, Grants etc.	all	
NAIA		
Number of Schools Offering Men's Track & Field	153	
Athletic Scholarships per School-Div I	12	
NJCAA		
Number of Schools Offering Men's Track & Field	78	
Athletic Scholarships per School	n/a	

Recruiting Opportunities & Evaluation Standards—
Women's Track
6.6% from High School to College

Collegiate Women's Track & Field Opportunities NCAA Division I		Track Websites
Number of Schools Offering Women's Track & Field	307	*www.dyestat.com* *www.track-and-field.net* *www.usatf.org* *www.trackinfo.org*
Athletic Scholarships per School	18	
NCAA Division II		
Number of Schools Offering Women's Track & Field	174	**Evaluation Standard**
Athletic Scholarships per School	12.6	Event Times & Measurements
NCAA Division III		
Number of Schools Offering Women's Track & Field	274	
Academic, Need, Merit, Grants etc.	all	
NAIA		
Number of Schools Offering Women's Track & Field	158	
Athletic Scholarships per School-Div I	12	
NJCAA		
Number of Schools Offering Women's Track & Field	82	
Athletic Scholarships per School	n/a	

Recruiting Opportunities & Evaluation Standards—
Men's Volleyball

Collegiate Men's Volleyball Opportunities NCAA Division I		Volleyball Websites
		www.avca.org
Number of Schools Offering Men's Volleyball	22	*www.volleyball.com*
		www.volleyball.org
Athletic Scholarships per School	4.5	*www.cvu.com*
NCAA Division II		*www.usavolleyball.org*
Number of Schools Offering Men's Volleyball	13	**Evaluation Standard**
Athletic Scholarships per School	4.5	Jump Touch
NCAA Division III		Defensive Ability
		Ball handling Skills
Number of Schools Offering Men's Volleyball	47	Quickness
		Agility
Academic, Need, Merit, Grants etc.	all	Block Touch
NAIA		Approach Touch
Number of Schools Offering Men's Volleyball	22	
Athletic Scholarships per School-Div I	4.5	
NJCAA		
Number of Schools Offering Men's Volleyball	n/a	
Athletic Scholarships per School	n/a	

Recruiting Opportunities & Evaluation Standards—
Women's Volleyball
5.6% from High School to College

Collegiate Women's Volleyball Opportunities NCAA Division I	
Number of Schools Offering Women's Volleyball	317
Athletic Scholarships per School	12
NCAA Division II	
Number of Schools Offering Women's Volleyball	276
Athletic Scholarships per School	8
NCAA Division III	
Number of Schools Offering Women's Volleyball	423
Academic, Need, Merit, Grants etc.	all
NAIA	
Number of Schools Offering Women's Volleyball	242
Athletic Scholarships per School-Div I	8
NJCAA	
Number of Schools Offering Women's Volleyball	299
Athletic Scholarships per School	n/a

Volleyball Websites

www.avca.org
www.volleyball.com
www.volleyball.org
www.cvu.com
www.usavolleyball.org

Evaluation Standard

Jump Touch
Defensive Ability
Ball handling Skills
Quickness
Agility
Block Touch
Approach Touch

Recruiting Opportunities & Evaluation Standards—
Men's Water Polo
6.9 % from High School to College

Collegiate Men's Water Polo Opportunities NCAA Division I	
Number of Schools Offering Men's Water Polo	22
Athletic Scholarships per School	4.5
NCAA Division II	
Number of Schools Offering Men's Water Polo	5
Athletic Scholarships per School	4.5
NCAA Division III	
Number of Schools Offering Men's Water Polo	15
Academic, Need, Merit, Grants etc.	all

Recruiting Opportunities & Evaluation Standards—
Women's Water Polo
8.1% from High School to College

Collegiate Women's Water Polo Opportunities	
NCAA Division I	
Number of Schools Offering Women's Water Polo	32
Athletic Scholarships per School	8
NCAA Division II	
Number of Schools Offering Women's Water Polo	7
Athletic Scholarships per School	8
NCAA Division III	
Number of Schools Offering Women's Water Polo	20
Academic, Need, Merit, Grants etc.	all

Recruiting Opportunities & Evaluation Standards—
Wrestling
3.4% from High School to College

Collegiate Wrestling Opportunities	
NCAA Division I	
Number of Schools Offering Wrestling	22
Athletic Scholarships per School	4.5
NCAA Division II	
Number of Schools Offering Wrestling	5
Athletic Scholarships per School	4.5
NCAA Division III	
Number of Schools Offering Wrestling	15
Academic, Need, Merit, Grants etc.	all
NAIA	
Number of Schools Offering Wrestling	242
Athletic Scholarships per School-Div I	8
NJCAA	
Number of Schools Offering Wrestling	299
Athletic Scholarships per School	n/a

Wrestling Websites
www.nwcaonline.com
www.ncwa.net
www.themat.com
www.intermatwrestle.com
www.ameteurwrestler.com

Glossary of Athletic Recruiting Terms

Contact: A contact occurs any time a coach has any face-to-face contact with you or your parents off the college's campus and says more than hello.

Contact period: During this time, a college coach may have in-person contact with you and/or your parents on or off the college's campus. The coach may also watch you play or visit your high school.

Dead period: A college coach may not have any in-person contact with you or your parents on or off campus at any time during a dead period. The coach may write and telephone you or your parents during this time.

Evaluation: An evaluation is an activity by a coach to evaluate your academic or athletics ability. This would include visiting your high school or watching you practice or compete.

Evaluation Period: During this time, a college coach may watch you play or visit your high school, but cannot have any in-person conversations with you or your parents off the college's campus. You and your parents can visit a college campus during this period. A coach may write and telephone you or your parents during this time.

National Letter of Intent: The National Letter of Intent (NLI) is a voluntary program administered by the Eligibility Center. By signing an NLI, your son or daughter agrees to attend the institution for one academic year. In exchange, that institution must provide athletic financial aid for one academic year.

Official visit: Any visit to a college campus by you and your parents paid for by the college. The college may pay all or some of the following expenses: Your transportation to and from the college, room and meals (three per day) while you are visiting the college, reasonable entertainment expenses; including three complimentary admissions to a home athletics contest. Before a college may invite you on an official visit, you will have to provide the college with a copy of your high school transcript, (Division I only) SAT, ACT or PLAN score, and register with the Eligibility Center.

Prospective student-athlete: You become a "prospective student-athlete" when: You start ninth-grade classes; or before your ninth-grade year, a college gives you, your relatives or your friends any financial aid or other benefits that the college does not generally provide to students.

Quiet period: During this time, a college coach may not have any in-person contact with you or your parents off the college's campus. The coach may not watch you play or visit your high school during this period. You and your parents may visit a college campus during this time. A coach may write or telephone you or your parents during this time.

Unofficial visit: Any visit by you and your parents to a college campus paid for by you or your parents. The only expense you may receive from the college is three complimentary admissions to a home athletics contest. You may make as many unofficial visits as you like and may take those visits at any time. The only time you cannot talk with a coach during an unofficial visit is during a dead period.

Verbal commitment: This phrase is used to describe a college bound student-athlete's commitment to a school before he or she signs (or is able to sign) a National Letter of Intent. A college bound student-athlete can announce a verbal commitment at any time. While verbal commitments have become very popular for both college-bound student-athletes and coaches, this "commitment" is NOT binding by either the college-bound student-athlete or the institution. Only the signing of the National Letter of Intent accompanied by a financial aid agreement is binding on both parties.

SECTION II

Student-Athlete Career Education

In this section you will learn the following:

- ➢ Who to speak with to discuss careers & majors
- ➢ Challenges facing college graduates for jobs & careers
- ➢ Where the job opportunities are expected to be over the next four years
- ➢ How to investigate the right career for you
- ➢ What opportunities are available in the military

The quality of a person's life is in direct proportion to their commitment to excellence, regardless of their chosen field of endeavor.

—Vince Lombardi

The purpose of life is not to win. The purpose of life is to grow and to share. When you come to look back on all that you have done in life, you will get more satisfaction from the pleasure you have brought to other people's lives than you will from the times that you out-did or defeated them.

—Rabbi Harold Kushner

Talk to your High School Counselor

Tell your counselor you are interested in playing college sports so that they can assess the courses you are currently taking and determine what additional courses you need to take to be eligible to sign a letter of intent and attend college on a scholarship. Furthermore, your counselor will provide you with dates to take the ACT/SAT and begin discussion on what careers you would like to pursue beyond the athletic realm. Also your counselor will have insight on all college fairs and practice ACT workshops. College counselors are full of information. Do not be afraid to ask your counselor what they know about particular universities and which universities may have a history of admitting players with low academic scores. It is not realistic to believe you can meet with your counselor 5-6 times a year. However, it is imperative you and your family meet with the counselor once a year and discuss what you need and can do to give yourself the best chance to be eligible to play college sports and what are your options are in case you fall short. If your counselor is just not a good fit or does not have the time to work with you, there are other options. There are many education consultants that you can speak with.

Independent Educational Consultants Association (703) 591-4850
National Association for College Admissions Counselors (800) 822-6285

This should be the last option considering you could try to get a new counselor at your high school. Career and educational consultants can be expensive and most colleges will not use their recommendations.

In raising the bar in student-athlete career education, Noblesteps Management is one of very few athletic recruiting companies that offer career education for student-athletes. Student-athletes are performers who thrive to do their trade well within and outside the sports realm. Therefore Noblesteps Management recognizes how important application is to student-athletes and provides the practical approach to assist student-athletes in establishing a vision for what their career could entail and empowering them to pursue it. Go to *www.noblesteps.com* to learn more on career education for student-athletes.

Advice from Student-Athlete Human Resource Director—Jeantique Richardson

"Nobody gave me anything"! That was the first words out of Jeantique Richardson's mouth when I asked her about her life. That is an impressive statement considering in high school Jeantique was a three time All State volleyball player in high school out of Albuquerque, New Mexico and inducted into the New Mexico High School Hall of Fame. However, she did not allow her competitive ambitions affect her perception of her education and athletic career. From a recruiting perspective, Jeantique worked with her high school and club coaches to get the exposure she needed, however her focus was to never underestimate the need for receiving an education in the recruiting process. She recalls that it was the most important decision she made in her life. She wanted to make sure she went to a college that was graduating its student-athletes and not only using them as work horses for their athletic program. Jeantique's focus was simple, "Be prepared for the sport to end". Wow, Jeantique was a three time all state volleyball player and two time all star player in high school with the attitude that with all the success on the volleyball court did not underestimate the importance of education and career after athletics. Miss Richardson kept her focus throughout college. She graduated with a degree in psychology and earned a Masters in Human Resource Development. To find her career path, Jeantique did not depend on her university. She interviewed informally with more than 50 professionals about their jobs, applied her psychology to business, and pursued and completed her Master's Degree program. Jeantique communicated that it is important for student-athletes to know that the job market is very, very competitive. She says, "Don't expect someone to give you a job because you graduated from an under-graduate school with a degree." Currently, she is a human resource director where entry level jobs are being applied for by applicants with 15-20 years experience with an MBA, a track record of hard work and dedication vs. college graduates with a degree and high expectations that her company owes them something. Jeantique says, "Who do you think I am going to hire?"

Five Serious Job Trends Affecting College Graduates

Trend 1: *More students' today are graduating with a College Degree than ever before*

According to the National Center of Education Statistics 935,000 students in 1980 and 1.4 million students in 2005 graduated with a bachelor's degree. The United States is becoming increasingly crowded with unemployed college graduates and very competitive with tenured college graduates with college degrees. Most companies offer "tuition reimbursement" to its employees compounded with online and accelerated degree programs. Ceridian Corporation reported in a 2005 study of 1000 major US employers that 78% of companies provided educational assistance options to their workforce, with nearly 75% specifically offering tuition reimbursement. As a result, the number of college graduates continues to keep pace with inflation.

Trend 2: *Surplus of misguided college graduates*

The first investment a student makes after high school for their future is often a college education. According to a study done by collegeboard, the cost of college from 2006-2007 rose 6.3% for private schools and 6.6% for public schools with an average of $32,307.00 and $13,587 respectively for tuition, fees and room and board. The study says students that switched schools and majors usually completed college within six years with a cost of $85,522 at a public university and $193,842 at a private university. The National Center of Education Statistics reports that 40% of college graduates in 2007 not enrolled in graduate school were working in jobs that did not require a college education. This is a disturbing statistic because it says that if 1.4 million people graduated with a degree, 560,000 had jobs with lower pay than expected and were frustrated that the system was not paying off. Is this the high school or college counselors fault? Well, high school counselors are so inundated with up to 300 schedules and special needs youth, that they don't have the time to career coach. Furthermore, they don't have the tools to constructively identify interests and preferences at any depth. Joan Kroll, Director of Career Services, Bowling Green University says, "Career education is vital for success. Never before have American workers needed to be self-directed and self-managing. It is a collective approach to making students succeed". So, when should students begin career education and plan activities to build their resume? Noblesteps Management conducted a survey of career directors and found the following:

When asked of university Career Directors nationwide, "What year do you favor to begin career planning?" **75%** favored the junior year and **10%** favored the senior year in high school. Only **15% favored a student's freshman year in college!**

Greg Ip, writer with The Wall Street Journal says, "College workers are more *plentiful*, more *commoditized* and more subject to the downsizing that used to be the purview of blue collar workers only."

Harvard University economists, Lawrence Katz and Claudia Goldin argue that in the 1990's, it became easier for firms to do overseas, or with computers at home, the work once done by, "lower-end college graduates in middle management and certain professional positions." The strategy to compete for employment in the 21st Century revolves around self-awareness, self-development and self-management.

Dr. Kimberley Beyer, Director of Career Services for Akron University says, "Students need to know themselves and take self-assessments to understand who they are and what they bring to the table, including their goals and dreams." This is a scary trend because a college education once meant you were a big fish in a little pond, now means you are a small fish in a school of fish who are confused on which way to go.

Trend 3: *Chest deep in Debt after college*

An analysis by Experian showed that from 2004-2005 lenders provided 14 Billion in private loans, an increase of 734% from a decade earlier. These college loans carry higher interest rates and have less flexible payment options than federal student loans. Tuition has risen over the past 3 decades 268% & 248% for public and private universities respectively. A recent study by the National Center of Education Statistics reports that 50% of college students have an average of $10,000 in student loans. The number of people between the ages of 22-29 has increased their debt load 10% to an average of $16,120 according to Experian; this includes student loan and credit card debt. Furthermore, the fastest growing segment with student loan debts are those with debt of $20,000 or more, that's up from 1.7% in 2001 to 3% in 2006. Debt has become such a burden that a survey showed that 58% of twenty something's it surveyed moved back home after college and 32% of those stayed for more than a year.

Trend 4: *A Surplus of Unemployed College Graduates*

There are 16 million total unemployed workers in America, according to the Bureau of Labor Statistics as of October 2009. As I am writing this manuscript, the Bureau of Labor Statistics reports unemployment rose to 10.2, the highest since 1983. 5.6 million Of unemployed workers have been unemployed for 27 weeks (6-months). A survey by nonprofit Project on Student Debt performed a survey that reflected that unemployment for recent graduates between 20-24 years old was 10.6% the highest ever recorded. The Student Association for Voter Empowerment reports that students from the ages 16-24 have an unemployment rate of 19%.

Trend 5: *Inefficient Career Exploration Habits*

The average college graduate finishes their bachelor degree in 4.2 years according to collegeboard.com. When students change their major or school, the average time to complete their education hikes to an astounding 6.2 years! A Career Director at a major university told me that students often enter college and have no idea what a career is. College is a quarter life crises for them. In the Noblesteps study, **90**% of respondents said students switched majors between 1-3 times, astoundingly, **10**% said students switched up to **4** times. One career director who asked to stay anonymous says, "Student's enter college to find out who they are." Unfortunately, in our economy with the trends that are facing our graduates, this could mean you earn a degree in a misguided fashion, with a mountain of debt and inefficient career exploration and network habits, competing for employment against millions of experienced and college educated job searchers.

~The Yoga Sutras of Patanjali "When you are inspired by some great purpose, some extraordinary project, all your thoughts break their bounds. Your mind transcends limitations your conscious expands in every direction and you find yourself in a new great and wonderful world."

College & Career Planning Resources

Planning a career for many student-athletes is sometimes 80% doing something you enjoy, and 20% default. Meaning, if you are in college volunteering to do jobs you enjoy that compliment your education, then as a result finding yourself taking part in a career that is fun and sometimes as fulfilling as playing the sport you love. Following are a list of resources that will help you find meaning in your career development activities:

❖ The College Board: *www.collegeboard.com/*
❖ The Sallie Mae Fund: *www.collegeanswer.com*
❖ AZ Commission for Postsecondary Education: *www.azhighered.org*
❖ CollegeNET: *www.collegenet.com*
❖ Collegequest: *www.collegequest.com*
❖ Career One Stop: *www.careerinfonet.org*
❖ Princeton Review: *www.review.com*
❖ US News & World Reports: *www.usnews.com*
❖ Social Life: *www.collegenews.com*
❖ Writing College Essays: *www.essayedge.com*
❖ Test U: *www.testu.com*
❖ School Safety Records: *www.ope.ed.gov/security*
❖ College Preparation: *www.ed.gov/studentaid*
❖ Petersons Entrance Exam Prep: *www.petersons.com*
❖ College bound for freshman: *www.collegebound.net*
❖ Market Yourself for admissions: *www.collegeapps.com*
❖ Customized Admissions Applications: *www.collegenet.com*
❖ College Search: *www.collegelink.com*
❖ Plan your future after college: *www.mapping-your-future.org*
❖ Career Advice Center: *www.careers.org*

There is no easy way to make a decision on what major to choose in college and how it will ultimately materialize into a career. Myers Briggs Type Indicator and the Strong Interest Explorer offer a high school/college career report through CPP.com. It is best to take these personality assessments under the instruction of a career coach to insure you understand the results of the tests. The questions on the assessment encompasses over 50 years of surveying of personality information that is gender specific and provides clear descriptions as to why certain occupations more than likely fit the personality of test takers. The career report also suggests majors, extra-curricular activities, and most and least likely career options. The US Department of Labor Statistics also publishes its estimated top occupations from 2006-2016 as follows:

Bachelor's Degree: Top Job Openings 2006-2016

Occupation Source: U.S. Bureau of Labor Statistics	Total Job Openings 2006-2016
Elementary school teachers, except special education	545,000
Accountants and auditors	450,000
Secondary school teachers, except special and vocational education	368,000
Computer software engineers, applications	300,000
Computer systems analysts	280,000
Middle school teachers, except special and vocational education	217,000
Network systems and data communications analysts	193,000
Securities, commodities, and financial services sales agents	161,000
Network and computer systems administrators	154,000
Construction managers	152,000

Green Job Sectors

Green Job Categories Source: Global Insights	Number in US Economy
Renewable Power Generation	127,246
Agriculture & Forestry	57,246
Construction & Systems Installation	8,741
Manufacturing	60,699
Equipment Dealers & Wholesalers	6,205
Engineering, Legal, Research & Consulting	418,715
Government	71,900

Career paths for aspiring student-athletes are often a distant thought and low on the priority list. However, when you consider many employers provide job training, it may not seem like an important piece of the life puzzle beyond completing a degree in a particular area of interest. However, with competition increasing for those training opportunities, it would be helpful to begin a career with the correct choice of majors and relevant job experience with skills that transfer and differentiate student-athletes from other applicants. The job market is becoming exceptionally competitive since more people are completing degrees than ever before with an increase in minorities graduating college and older adults in their 40-50's graduating with degrees. Additionally, there is an increase in businesses providing tuition reimbursement. There are five serious job trends that should be understood and taken into account when picking majors and pursuing career paths. It can be helpful to grab the yellow pages, a contact list of family and friends and interview as many people in the above occupations as possible to determine what they like about their careers. Following is a list of interview questions that could be helpful in assisting you in identifying and determining professions beyond the athletic realm that can be fulfilling to you in a future career.

10 Career Exploration Questions for Interviewing Professionals

Name of Professional _____

1. What do you do in a typical day?

2. What do you like the most about your work?

3. What do you find the most challenging?

4. What education is necessary? Is there on-the-job training?

5. What work experience/background is necessary and/or useful to do this job?

6. In your opinion, what is the job outlook in this career area in the global economy?

7. What are other specialties/areas in this occupation?

8. Where else could I find people involved in this field and can I contact you in the future?

9. What is the entry level position in this career?

10. Can you suggest any volunteer activities related to this type of work?

Uncle SAM Military Education Options

ARMY: US Military Academy, NY

Division—ROTC
Offer: Full Scholarship (tuition, books, and fees): stipend up to $400 per month while in school
Your Responsibility: Four years active duty, four years reserve duty
I ROTC class per semester: weekly drills
Qualifications: SAT 920: ACT 19: Age 17-21
Contact Info: 800-USA-ROTC: *www.goarmy.com*

Division—Active GI Bill
Offer: Up to $32,400 for college after discharge, Army College fund up to 50K in various military job areas, student loan repayment up to 65K, 75% tuition assistance during service
Your Responsibility: At least two years of active duty, $1200 contribution per 12 months towards benefit
Qualifications: High School Diploma or equivalent: Age 17-35
Contact Info: 800-USA-ARMY: *www.goarmy.com*

Division—Reserve GI Bill
Offer: Up to $9,936 for college after discharge, loan repayment up to $20,000
Your Responsibility: One weekend/month, two weeks/year for six years
Qualifications: High School Diploma or equivalent: age 17-35
Contact Info: 800-USA-ARMY: *www.goarmy.com*

Division—Guard GI Bill
Offer: Up to $9,936 over 36 months, 75% tuition assistance, all states offer other tuition assistance programs
Your Responsibility: Three-six years enlistment, one weekend/month, two weeks/year
Qualifications: High School Diploma or equivalent
Info: 800-GO-GUARD

NAVY: US Naval Academy, Annapolis, MD

Division—ROTC
Offer: Full Scholarship (tuition, books, fees), stipend up to $400 per month while in school
Your Responsibility: Three years active duty, five years reserve duty
Qualifications: SAT 1050, ACT 22, Age: 18-34
Contact Info: 800-NAV-ROTC: *www.nrotc.navy.mil*

Division—Active GI Bill
Offer: Up to $28,800, some navel jobs through Navy College Fund, up to 15K, 75% tuition assistance up to $3,500, seaman-to-admiral (STA) 10K, tuition repayment up to 10K
Your Responsibility: At least two-six years of active duty, $1200 contribution per 12 months towards benefit (STA: 5 years active duty upon commissioning)
Qualifications: High School Diploma or equivalent, Age: 18-34, (STA: SAT 1000, ACT 21)
Contact Info: 800-USA-NAVY: *www.navyjobs.com*

Division—Reserve GI Bill
Offer: Up to $9,936 for college after discharge, loan repayment up to $20,000
Your Responsibility: One weekend/month, two weeks/year for four-six years active duty
Qualifications: High School Diploma or equivalent, Age: 21-38
Contact Info: 866-NAVRESI: *www.navalreserve.com*

MARINES

Division—ROTC
Offer: Full Scholarship (tuition, books, fees), stipend up to $200 per month while in school
Your Responsibility: Four-Six years active duty
Qualifications: SAT 1050, ACT 22, Age: 18-34
Contact Info: 800-MARINES: *www.marines.com*

Division—Active GI Bill
Offer: Up to $28,800 after discharge, 100% tuition assistance
Your Responsibility: At least three-five years of active duty, $1200 contribution
Qualifications: High School Diploma or equivalent
Contact Info: 800-MARINES: *www.marines.com*

Division—Reserve GI Bill
Offer: Up to $7,124.40 for college after discharge
Your Responsibility: One weekend/month, two weeks/year for six years
Qualifications: High School Diploma or equivalent
Contact Info: 800-MARINES: *www.marines.com*

AIR FORCE—U.S. Air Force Academy, Colorado Springs, CO

Division—ROTC
Offer: Full Scholarship, books up to $510/year, stipend up to $400 per month while in school
Your Responsibility: Four years active duty
Qualifications: SAT 1100, ACT 24
Contact Info: 866-4AFROTC: *www.afrotc.com*

Division—Active GI Bill
Offer: Up to $40,000 after discharge, 100% tuition assistance up to $4500 per year, college credit for training, loan repayment up to $10,000
Your Responsibility: At least four-six years of active duty, $1200 contribution plus, $600 to increase benefit by $5,400
Qualifications: High School Diploma or equivalent
Contact Info: 800-423-USAF: *www.airforce.com*

Division—Reserve GI Bill
Offer: Up to $9,936, more for various jobs, 100% tuition assistance to $4,500/year during service
Your Responsibility: One weekend/month, two weeks/year for six years
Qualifications: High School Diploma or equivalent
Contact Info: 800-257-121: *www.afreserve.com*

United States Coast Guard—New London, CT

Division—Selected Reserve Guard GI Bill
Offer: Up to $9,036, state National Guard units put forward supplementary tuition assistance and loan repayment benefits
Your Responsibility: Three-six years enlistment, one weekend/month, two weeks/year
Qualifications: High School Diploma or equivalent
Contact Info: 800-TO-GO-ANG: *www.af.mil*

Division—ROTC—No ROTC; College Student Commissioning Program for qualifying minority students
Offer: $1,200/month during last two years
Your Responsibility: Three years active duty
Qualifications: SAT 1100, ACT 21, GPA 2.5
Contact Info: 877-NOW-USCG: *www.gocoastguard.com*

Division—Active GI Bill
Offer: up to $28,000
Your Responsibility: Four-six years active duty, two-four years reserve duty, $1,200 contribution
Qualifications: High School Diploma or equivalent
Contact Info: 877-NOW-USCG: *www.gocoastguard.com*

Division—Reserve GI Bill
Offer: Up to $9,936 for college after discharge, loan repayment up to $20,000
Your Responsibility: One weekend/month, two weeks/year for four years
Qualifications: High School Diploma or equivalent
Contact Info: 800-424-8883: *www.uscg.mil*

Be sure to check all websites and confirm information and/or adjustments

Glossary of Career Education Terms

Assessment: Comparing individual career performance to predetermined standards.

Career: A lifestyle concept that involves a sequence of work in which one engages throughout a lifetime. Careers are unique to each person; dynamic and unfolding throughout life.

Career Branding: Branding is your reputation. Branding is about building a name for yourself, showcasing what sets you apart from other job-seekers, and describing the added value you bring to an employer.

Career Coach: Also called career consultant, career adviser, work-life coach, personal career trainer, and life management facilitator. These professionals have been likened to personal trainers for your life/career, serving the role as your champion, cheerleader, advocate, mentor, partner, and sounding board on all issues related to your job or career search.

Career Exploration: A person's involvement in trying out a variety of activities, roles, and situations in order to learn more about aptitude for or interest in an occupation or other career opportunities.

Career Paths: Clusters of occupations/careers that are combined together because the people in them share similar interests and strengths. All paths include a variety of occupations requiring different levels of education and training.

Career Planning: Determining a suitable career path using knowledge of personal interests, skills and preferred futures (dreams), researching the educational and skill requirements of a variety of potential work and life roles. Career planning is the continuous process of evaluating your current lifestyle, likes/dislikes, passions, skills, personality, dream job, current job and career path, and making corrections and improvements to better prepare for future steps in your career, as needed, or to make a career change.

Cover Letter: The letter that accompanies a CV or resume. It may be a motivation letter or just a brief note to attach the resume. It should always accompany your resume when you contact a potential employer. A good cover letter opens a window to your personality (and describes specific strengths and skills you offer the employer). It should entice the employer to read your resume.

CV Curriculum Vitae: A special type of resume traditionally used within the academic community. Earned degrees, teaching and research experience, publications, presentations, and related activities are featured. Unlike a resume, a CV tends to be longer and more informational than promotional in tone.

Human Resources: The department dealing with recruiting and further management of personnel matters. The human resources function provides critical support and advice to the management. The attraction, retention and development of high caliber people are a source of competitive advantage and are the responsibility of HR departments.

Internship: A one-on-one relationship that provides for "hands-on" learning in the area of the student's career interest. A learning contract outlines the expectations and responsibilities of both parties. Employers provide structured work experiences that include workplace readiness and job-specific skill development that connect to school-based learning. Ideally, students work in a number of departments or positions during their internships so they can have a better career-oriented experience.

Job Satisfaction: A term to describe how content an individual is with his or her job. It includes many factors, including the work itself, value to the organization, impact on organization, compensation, and more. When workers are very unhappy with their jobs, they suffer both mentally and physically.

Job Shadowing: A student observes the daily routine of an employee and then "interviews" the employee about his/her work and education. This kind of activity is conducted just after the student has finished his or her degree program, and prior to starting a career.

Mentor: Experiences which link student-athletes with a local business/industry/community-based individual. Activities may focus on school-related activities or may target those who need support outside the school setting.

Mentors are encouraged to support the development of academic skills and provide guidance on career-related, interdisciplinary projects, and workplace culture.

Mentoring: Mentoring is a formal relationship between a coach with significant experience (mentor) and a student-athlete (mentee) where each develops professionally through the transfer of experience and the opportunity to seek alternative perspectives.

Resume: A document containing a summary or listing of relevant job experience and education, usually for the purpose of securing a new job. Often the first item a potential employer encounters regarding the job seeker, and therefore a large amount of importance is often ascribed to it.

Skills: The learned abilities and knowledge which must be developed for successful job performance.

SECTION III

Financial Aid Education

In this section you will learn the following:

✓   Managing the college preparation process

Discipline is doing what you would rather not do so that you can do what you would rather do

In the final analysis, the one quality that all successful people have . . . is the ability to take on responsibility

—Michael Korda

Cost of Attendance

Athletic scholarships are not the only scholarships available! There are vast opportunities available to investigate as well. The bigger the aid package the less student loans you will need!

Cost of Attendance

1) Tuition and Fees
2) Room & Board
3) Books & Supplies
4) Personal Expenses
5) Transportation

It is suggested as you travel through this process to maintain good records. The records pertaining to how much you are expected to pay out-of-pocket is especially important because surprises have derailed many student-athletes. Following is a worksheet developed to assist in calculating your financial aid packages, scholarship aid, and loans.

Cost of Attendance Calculations

Cost of Attendance Calculations				
	College #1	College #2	College #3	College #4
College Name	Division III College			
Amount Athletic Scholarship	$ -			
Amount of Academic Scholarship #1	$ 15,000.00			
Amount Of Academic Scholarship #2	$ 8,000.00			
Amount of Grants (Federal Aid)	$ 6,500.00			
Total Financial Aid Award	$ 29,500.00	$ -	$ -	$ -
Cost of Tuition	$ (34,950.00)			
Cost of Room & Board	$ (8,950.00)			
est. Cost of Books & Supplies	$ (900.00)			
Estimated Miscellaneous Expenses	$ (700.00)			
Total Cost of Attendance	$ (45,500.00)	$ -	$ -	$ -
"Out of Pocket" Costs per year	$ (16,000.00)	$ -	$ -	$ -

The example above is for a Division III School that provides a much esteemed education. Considering the above example, the school does not offer athletic scholarships; however, they provide a Financial Aid Award package that consists of various scholarships and need-based aid to cover the cost of attendance. In the end, this student would be responsible for getting loans in excess of $16,000 per year. This is why it can be helpful to focus on three to four schools and compare the "out of pocket" or loans that you will be responsible for per year. Therefore, you can negotiate between the colleges on what aid packages they are offering and leverage one of the schools if they want you badly enough to come to the table with a more robust financial aid award.

Financial Need

Cost of Attendance (COA)
- Expected Family Contribution (EFC)
= Financial Need

Online Financial Aid Resources

Beyond an athletic scholarship, there are other forms of aid available (Loans, Grants, Merit Scholarships and Work Study) and can be researched through the following websites:

- ✓ Free Application for financial student aid: *www.fafsa.ed.gov*
- ✓ All Scholar—free scholarship searches: *www.allscholar.com*
- ✓ Fast web—Scholarship & College Search: *www.fastweb.com*
- ✓ Finaid—student guide to financial aid: *www.finaid.org*
- ✓ College Goal Sunday: *www.collegegoalsundayusa.org/*
- ✓ Us Department of Education: *www.ed.gov/studentaid*
- ✓ Sallie Mae Private loans: *www.wiredscholar.com*
- ✓ Scholarship Finder: *www.scholarships.com*
- ✓ National Student Loan Data System: *www.nslds.ed.gov*
- ✓ Chela Financial: *www.loans4students.org*
- ✓ Nel Net: *www.nelnet.net*
- ✓ Students.gov: *www.students.gov*
- ✓ Free Scholarship Guide over 4000 scholarships available: *www. freescholarshipguide.com*

The aforementioned is a small sample of how lucrative the opportunities can be. In a perfect world, your athletic and academic achievements will produce a scholarship that covers all your college expenses and more!!! However, that is not always the case and it will therefore be important to understand the other various forms of aid that may include different types of loans, grants, forms, work programs, and measurements that you will need to be aware of and understand.

Senior Year Financial Aid Timeline

August

- ✓ Request applications and information from colleges.
- ✓ Make unofficial visits throughout the fall to help narrow your choices.

September

- ✓ Plan for college fairs and admissions representatives' visits and meeting with the school counselor to develop a college admissions plan.
- ✓ Register for the SAT or the ACT. Investing in a preparation course for either test may help you to become more comfortable with the testing process and to perform better on the exam.

October

- ✓ Create a schedule of admissions and financial aid deadlines.
- ✓ Work on completing college applications and essays.
- ✓ Request transcripts and letters of recommendation from coaches, counselors, teachers, etc.
- ✓ Explore college or scholarship information or apply to colleges online (some campuses may charge an extra fee; however, some campuses waive fees, since online applications speed up processing).

November

- ✓ Follow up with your high school guidance counselor to ensure that letters of recommendation are submitted.
- ✓ Perform your final revisions to essays and applications.

December

✓ Submit and maintain a personal file for college applications.

✓ Investigate all financial aid forms that may be required by your target schools.

January

✓ Obtain a Free Application for Federal Student Aid (FAFSA) from your school counselor or through the Department of Education (DOE). To complete the FAFSA, you will need your family's (estimated) income tax information for the year. Your parents should complete taxes early to help in filling out the FAFSA. Keep a copy of this information, as some officials may request to see it later.

✓ Complete the FAFSA online or fill out, photocopy, and then submit it by mail.

February

✓ Contact the college's financial aid office to see if financial aid programs exist on a state or campus level. Submit all the necessary paperwork or applications for any private or outside scholarships you may have identified in October.

✓ Be sure that you have submitted all required forms: the college admissions application, the FAFSA, any private scholarship applications, and any state or campus forms required for financial aid programs outside the federal student aid programs.

March

✓ Ask your high school counselor about Advanced Placement (AP) exams offered for college credit and about the cost of the exams. Contact the registrar's office at the college or school you plan to attend to find out what score is necessary to receive the college credit. If you will be taking an AP exam, consider starting an AP preparation course for the tests in May.

April

- ✓ Receive admissions notification(s).
- ✓ Compare your financial aid awards to cost of school attendance.
- ✓ Make a final enrollment decision and submit the enrollment deposit, if requested.
- ✓ Notify any schools that you have chosen not to attend that have accepted you that you will not be attending.
- ✓ Sign and return financial aid forms for the school you will be attending.

May

- ✓ Take any applicable Advanced Placement (AP) exams.
- ✓ Send final transcript and student loan application(s) to your chosen college.
- ✓ Contact the college's financial aid office to check your financial aid package status.

June

- ✓ Complete any remaining financial aid forms.
- ✓ Plan for college orientation, transportation, and housing.

July

- ✓ Finalize college transportation and housing for the fall.

Glossary of Financial Aid Terms

Academic Year: A period of at least 30 weeks of instructional time during which a full-time student is expected to complete at least 24 semester or trimester hours, or at least 36 quarter hours, at an institution that measures program length in credit hours; or at least 900 clock hours at an institution that measures program length in clock hours.

Award Letter: The official document, issued by the financial aid office, which lists all the financial aid awarded to the student. While award letters vary among institutions, the letter generally lists the expected family contribution, cost of attendance and all the terms of the aid awarded.

Consolidation: A loan program that allows a borrower to combine various educational loans into one new loan. By extending the repayment period (up to 30 years depending on the loan amount) and allowing a single monthly payment, consolidation can make loan repayment easier for some borrowers.

Cost of Attendance: The student's cost of attendance includes tuition, fees, and standard allocation designed to cover reasonable living expenses while attending school. The cost of attendance is determined by the school using guidelines established by federal regulations.

CSS Profile—College Scholarship Search Profile: Financial aid form for private colleges.

Default—Not repaying the loan according to the terms of the promissory note which will adversely affect your credit.

Deferment: An authorized period of time during which a borrower may postpone principal and interest payments. Deferments are available while borrowers are in school at least half time, enrolled in a graduate fellowship program or rehabilitation training program, and during periods of unemployment or economic hardship. Other deferments may be available depending on when and what you borrowed. Contact your lender for additional details.

EFC—Estimated Family Contribution: Based on FAFSA inputs, the government's calculation of what your family can afford to contribute to college expenses.

FAFSA—Free Application for Federal Student Aid: Determines your eligibility to receive financial aid.

Financial Aid Package: The total financial aid a student receives. Federal and non-federal aid such as grants, loans, work-study, and scholarships are combined in a "package" to help meet the student's need.

Financial Need: The difference between what it costs to attend a particular college and the amount it has been determined that a student and his/her family can afford to pay toward those expenses. The term "demonstrated financial need" is typically used to describe an assessment based on Institutional Methodology for undergraduate need-based, institutional funding.

Forbearance: An authorized period of time during which the lender agrees to temporarily postpone a borrower's principal repayment obligation. Interest continues to accrue and usually must be paid during the forbearance period. Forbearance may be granted at the lender's discretion when a borrower is willing to repay their loan but is unable to do so.

FWS—Federal Work Study: Awards college jobs to students to pay college expenses.

Grace Period—Loans provided have a six-nine month grace period after graduation or when you leave college.

Grant: Type of financial aid award based on need or merit that is not repaid by the student.

HEOP/EOP—Higher Education Opportunity Program: Educational and economical disadvantage aid for NY State.

Interest: A fee charged for the use of borrowed money. Interest is calculated as a percentage of the principal loan amount. The rate may be constant throughout the life of the loan (fixed rate) or it may change at specified times (variable rate).

Institutional Methodology: A nationally accepted standard used by many colleges, universities, graduate and professional schools, and private scholarship programs for assessing a family's financial eligibility to receive funding from the school to help meet the Cost of Attendance.

Merit Based Aid: Financial aid that is awarded based on a student's academic, leadership or artistic merit, or some other criteria, and does not depend on financial need. Merit-based awards may look at a student's grades, test scores, special talents, or extracurricular activities to determine eligibility.

Need Based Aid: Financial aid that is awarded based on a student's financial circumstance. Need-based aid can be awarded in the form of grants, loans, or work-study.

Pell Grants: Federal grants that range from $400 to $4,000 per academic based on financial need.

Promissory Note: A legal document that you sign for a loan that promises you will repay the loan.

SAR-Student Aid Report: Includes your EFC and is sent to colleges listed on FAFSA.

Subsidized Loans: Awarded on the basis of financial need whereas the federal government "subsidizes" the interest on the loan.

Unsubsidized Loans: With this loan, the government does not pay the interest while the student is enrolled.